"Our journey is what makes us who we are"

Enjoy
Sandra Pezzino

Sept 29, 2001

Three Small Pebbles

Three Small Pebbles

A Novel

Sandra Pezzino

Copyright © 2016 by Sandra Pezzino.

ISBN: Softcover   978-1-5144-2877-1
            eBook   978-1-5144-2876-4

All rights reserved. No part of this book may be reproduced or transmitted in any form or by any means, electronic or mechanical, including photocopying, recording, or by any information storage and retrieval system, without permission in writing from the copyright owner.

Any people depicted in stock imagery provided by Thinkstock are models, and such images are being used for illustrative purposes only.
Certain stock imagery © Thinkstock.

Print information available on the last page.

Rev. date: 01/28/2016

To order additional copies of this book, contact:
Xlibris
1-888-795-4274
www.Xlibris.com
Orders@Xlibris.com

CONTENTS

Chapter 1 1
Chapter 2 4
Chapter 3 7
Chapter 4 9
Chapter 5 12
Chapter 6 14
Chapter 7 18
Chapter 8 21
Chapter 9 27
Chapter 10 32
Chapter 11 34
Chapter 12 43
Chapter 13 47
Chapter 14 53
Chapter 15 57
Chapter 16 61
Chapter 17 64
Chapter 18 69
Chapter 19 72
Chapter 20 76
Chapter 21 84
Chapter 22 88
Chapter 23 95

Chapter 24 98
Chapter 25 105
Chapter 26 110
Chapter 27 116
Chapter 28 118
Chapter 29 125
Chapter 30 133
Chapter 31 137
Chapter 32 140
Chapter 33 145
Chapter 34 151
Chapter 35 155
Chapter 36 158
Chapter 37 162
Chapter 38 166
Chapter 39 169

Chapter 1

My name is Sandra. For many years I had been contemplating writing a remarkable story about a very special person in my life. She was not only special to me, but to anyone who came to know her. Actually, it was impossible not to love her once you spent a little time with her.

Her maiden name was Elza Zagars. She was my maternal grandmother. Nana, as I affectionately called her, was born in 1910 in Gulbene, Latvia. She married Arturs Nogobods. They had three children. My mother was their middle child. Like many first generation Americans, I wanted to visit my grandmother's hometown since I was a little child. My wish finally came true in 2001 after 42 years.

The primary purpose of our trip was to visit my grandparents' property in Gulbene, Latvia. I went with my mother, Inara Overfield, and my mother's sisters, Kitija and Olita. My cousins, Jesse, Edwin and Richard also decided to come and explore their heritage. I had no idea what to expect and didn't fully comprehend at the time how much of a life-changing event this would be. I was certain about one thing however, Gulbene wasn't going to be anything like where I grew up in West Seneca.

I was actually born in Presque Isle, Maine. My father, William Overfield, was in the U.S. Air Force at the time. Shortly after I was born, he moved his family to West Seneca, New York. As a child, I heard many stories about love, war, rebirth, triumph, and most importantly, my Latvian heritage. As I grew older, these stories became more intriguing to me. Needless to say, when the opportunity presented itself in 2001, there was no thinking twice about going.

Riga is the capital of Latvia. Its population is around 650,000 people. When we first arrived, I was overwhelmed by the city's beauty. There was color everywhere. The furniture was beautiful and unique. Even the curtains were colorful and unique. Latvians are also well-known for their weaving. I was amazed by the intricate designs, the dyes used, their insignias, and their exquisite quality. Even the flowers made an impact on me. There were flowers everywhere. The greatest impression however, was made by the Latvian people. I have never met a warmer group of people. Their need to please was second to none.

Riga is still a city in transition. While it is extremely beautiful, much is being restored at a painfully slow pace. One of the first things I saw was a man carrying long pieces of wood to a building under renovation. On the same street, I saw a man working on a thatched roof. He had to walk up a ladder to the roof with each bundle. Manpower was the only resource available.

Even though I was 42 years old at the time, I was like a wide-eyed child as we made our way through the countryside. We were about to visit my Nana and Papas' hometown of Gulbene. Every mile taught me something new. Every step I took was like a first-time experience. Truly, I was about to embark on my own experience of a lifetime.

Chapter 2

The countryside outside of the city of Riga is very beautiful. It is full of picturesque farms with many haystacks that had holes in the center. They looked like little houses. My mother told me that, while Nana and Papa worked, my mother and my aunts use to play in them. The countryside had many rolling hills full of incredibly beautiful birch trees. Those were Nana's favorites.

Along the way we stopped at a small store where the proprietor used beads to count up our purchases. I'll never forget the meat cookies that he had next to the cash register. These "pirags" were rolls with bacon inside of them. We grew up eating these. As we walked out of the store, we saw people transferring chickens from car to car.

Upon entering Gulbene, I got the impression it was a poor farm town. I suppose I had this impression because there were a lot of old and dilapidated Russian apartment buildings there. As we drove down the driveway to Nana's farmhouse, we could see a pond on the left that was full of ducks swimming about. Nana told me this was where she would wash her feet at night before going to bed. The pond was also surrounded by beautiful berry bushes.

My Nana grew quite a variety of berry bushes including raspberries, blackberries, currant berries, and a lot of other fruit bearing trees. She also grew some of the most beautiful flowers I have ever seen. The colors were spectacular. And in the distance to the east, one haystack after the other dotted the landscape.

As we approached the farmhouse, I couldn't believe this was Nana's childhood home. All of a sudden, Nana's relatives came running to greet us. Surprisingly, everyone knew my name. They started hugging and kissing me. I couldn't believe how excited these relatives were considering they had never met me before. They had been preparing for our arrival for weeks. I got a kick out of the shepherd mixes barking at us. They were told to go lay down, and they did. Even the dogs knew the language.

One of the nicest features of the farmhouse was the porch. It was small yet functional. Two rockers and a potted plant invited you to sit awhile and enjoy the view with a cup of hot tea. It reminded me of Nana and Papa's house in Orchard Park, New York.

The first impression I had of the interior of the farmhouse was of the kitchen. It was incredibly small but extremely efficient. I couldn't help reminiscing about Nana's kitchen around Christmastime. I could hear the ladies giving the men and children orders. The children were all very beautiful and obedient, and really shy. There was a stump next to the stove that Nana told us she used to sit on as a child while her mother was cooking.

Chapter 3

I suppose one could say the kitchen was the heart of any farmhouse. At its center was a stove with pots and pans. They were bubbling with mouthwatering aromas. One of the pots was clearly the largest pot I had ever seen.

I told one of the relatives that I would love to have that pot back home to make sauce with. She told me in Latvian (along with a lot of hand signals) that the pot was used to milk the cows. After she was finished using it to milk the cows, she would scrub the inside and outside really well, then cook with it. After she was done cooking with it, she would take it out to the barn to milk the cows all over again.

This was only one of the many things that reminded me of how easy our life is in the United States in comparison to theirs in Latvia. It certainly humbles you to think how life can be so difficult elsewhere. But one thing is most certain about these people: they are a proud group of people who love living a simple life.

After a good while in the kitchen, we decided to take a look at the garden. We pulled carrots out of the ground, and popped raspberries, blackberries, strawberries, and currants into our mouths. I had never seen gardens like this in my entire life. Every fruit and vegetable, along with every flower, looked like they belonged in a garden magazine. They were beyond perfect. None of the plants had one brown leaf or rotten berry for as far as the eye could see. In the distance you could hear the gentle whirring of the farm tractor going along between the haystacks. They resembled chess pieces perfectly spaced and waiting to make their next move.

That evening, I went to stay at Nana's niece's apartment in Gulbene. It was here, in this tiny kitchen, that I began putting my thoughts down on paper. More than ever, I realized that I came from very loving, hard-working, and honest people. I couldn't believe how difficult an existence they continue to endure. I suppose they do so because they are a very close-knit family. Instead of working independently of each other, they work together and share the same values and beliefs as a family unit. No one raises their voices. The children are polite and very respectful, and the women are friendly, extremely hard working, and sensitive to the needs of everyone in the family. Even the men take direction from the women. It is a simple existence.

Going to my grandmother's house for the first time was difficult in many ways. In some ways, it was a surreal experience. It was like walking into a painting that had been hung in my bedroom and now becoming a part of it. All the stories and experiences through the years of my life now made sense.

Chapter 4

I now began to understand things about my heritage in a new and exciting way. When I was very young, my grandfather would draw pictures of his house to show me what it was like. There was a brook on one side of the farmhouse and a bigger stream in the back of the property. These drawings would fuel my imagination. He would always finish the drawing with a bunny rabbit in the foreground. In some ways, I was that bunny rabbit.

As we drove up the road and surveyed his property, it was easy to see he had the most beautiful location in town. Trees lined both sides of the road. They came together to form a stunning canopy. There was a bus stop sign that indicated Kisu. My aunt said that was the nickname they gave to my grandfather's property. It now was a designated stop along the town's bus route.

At this point, we got out of the car and started walking up to the property line. I had a multitude of thoughts for every step I took. I found out that this was where the pick-up truck travelled when my grandparents' family was nearly taken away during the war. Papa had told me this was the dirt road where they fled with the few belongings they had to hide from the Russians. This was also the same dusty road where their two beloved dogs tried to follow them only to be told to go back home. Papa knew the dogs wouldn't be able to hide with them. It was hard for me to comprehend that this peaceful land was at one time anything but peaceful. It was full of turmoil.

As we got closer, we were told by one of the aunts that Papa and Nana's house had stood on a hill next to a large tree. Yet as far as the eye could see, there were no buildings. Instead, there were acres of fields that met up to a line of trees in the far distance. Only one tree stood strong and defiant. It was a tall tree next to where Papa and Nana's house had once stood. I was told Papa had planted this tree with his father as a young boy. At first glance we thought the old tree was dead, as it had several bare branches that hung at different levels. As I walked closer to get a better look, I found myself amazed at the sight of the beautiful, lush, green leaves that covered the top branches of the tree. Despite all that it had been through, this tree was not about to give in. When we told Nana this, she smiled and said, "Just like me!" At the base of this tree, there were three large boulders. My aunts told us these were all that were left of the foundation of Papa's house. We each took a small amount of dirt from near the foundation as a remembrance of our grandparents' struggle for survival.

Next, we walked to the side of the property where the brook had once been. It was dry now. Only rocks covered the bottom that gave us a hint of what direction it once travelled. My mother cried as we stood there admiring the blue forget-me-nots that lined the bank. Surely, she thought, the overwhelming beauty before us was a heaven-sent message from Papa.

Me posing near Papa's tree in 2001.

Chapter 5

Many years after visiting my grandparent's homeland I was enjoying an evening with my grandchildren. I was snuggling with my six year old grandson, Michael, on the couch. A coral fringed blanket was wrapped around our legs. My ten year old granddaughter, Cora, had just made a big bowl of buttered popcorn. I wasn't sure who enjoyed our Friday movie nights more. I secretly knew it was me. In all my life I'd never had anything that compared to these special times.

We were going through the movie listings, trying to find a movie that both my "littles" could agree on. After several minutes of uninteresting choices, my grandson said "Nonnie, why don't you tell us one of your stories!" I smiled thinking how easily he was pleased by my stories of long ago. I looked up at my grandaughter and she looked equally interested as she grabbed another hand full of buttered popcorn.

I asked, "Okay, what would you like to know about?" My grandson asked, "Nonnie, did you have a grandma?" Of course I did! Six year olds were so innocent.

I called my grandma, Nana. She was born in a far-away place called Latvia.

My Nana was your great-great grandmother! Her name was Elza Zagards. She was born in a very small clay bungalow on a German Baron's Estate, in Gulbene. They called the estate "Muiza." Her parents' names were Jule and Peters. They were very happy to have a little baby girl! She was the first and only girl after three sons. She had the most beautiful blond hair with curls and dimples! No one could agree on her eye color. It changed from blue to green depending on the lighting. Her three brothers, Volfrids, Vilhelm, and Arvids were each two years apart and very excited to have a little sister.

The family continued to work for the German Baron, taking care of his farmland in exchange for shelter and food. Latvia in 1910, when Nana was born, was under German occupation.

My little brown-eyed blonde grandson asked, "Nonnie, what does German Occupation mean?"

I said, "It means that they had to listen to the Germans tell them what to do as they made the rules. The Latvian people had to follow their laws. They weren't free like us."

He asked, "Why didn't they just come to Florida?" My granddaughter looked at me for an answer also.

"It wasn't that simple," I replied, "In fact you will see it was very, very hard."

Chapter 6

When Elza was two years old the German government made a new law. It said that all people in Latvia were entitled to their own land. They no longer could be kept like slaves. Soon after that little Elza and her family were given a small piece of property across the street from where she was born. This was very exciting for her family. They'd never had a place of their own. They built a small house and barn and called it "Pamati" meaning "the foundation." It was very small, but it was theirs. Elza shared her father and mother's room and her older brothers, Volfrids, Vilhelms, and Arvids shared a second room.

"Palmati" Zagars Family Photo.

Front row from left to right: Elza holding stroller; Elza's youngest brother, Arvids, is wearing glasses in a white shirt. Sitting next to him is her father, Peters. Her oldest brother, Volfrids, is sitting on the ground. Elza's mother, Jule, is holding a baby. Elza's middle brother, Vilhelms, is leaning against the house in dark jacket.

"Everyone adored their mother, Jule." She was kind and softhearted. They say that Elza was most like her; a very hard worker, wonderful baker and mother. The Zagards family worked hard to farm the land. As Elza grew older, their farm flourished. When she was 13, the farm was generating enough food, milk, and wheat to be self-sufficient. The days under German occupation had allowed an existence that had given them limited independence.

Elza was a bit of a dreamer. She often used her time alone to daydream. She was very shy and didn't know many girls her age. She once told me she washed her feet in the pond near the front of her house every night before going in for her nightly chores. It was her favorite time of the day. The sun was beginning to catch up with the horizon as she scattered crumbs of bread onto the pond's surface. Father, mother, and five ducklings would find their way to her, pushing their little webbed feet just as fast as they could go. The littlest one with his feathers appearing to be more disheveled than his siblings was always bringing up the rear. They were only too eager each night to share their fuzzy little family with her!

She dreamt of marrying someone tall with big strong shoulders, but sensitive and scholarly. They would live far from this small farm town. She didn't enjoy picking or planting rows and rows of fruits and vegetables, not to mention the cleaning of the barn. She hoped she would have lots of girls. She was far outnumbered as the only girl in her family.

"So did she?" My granddaughter blurted out.

"Well, not exactly…," I replied.

Her mother had encouraged her to join the school chorus. This was truly intimidating for her. She was so shy, and the idea of standing in the front… where every mistake could be heard, scared her to her core. Her older brother, Volfrids, had a wonderful voice. He was confident and a bit pushy. He walked Elza into the chorus room to introduce her and announce that she would be joining their singing group! At age thirteen, she was among the youngest in the group. There were students and non-students alike up to the age of eighteen. As feared, she was placed in the front row. It was in this music group that she first noticed she'd caught the attention of Arturs Nogobods. She told me he was everything she was not. He was five years older than she and as confidant as they come. She said it had only been the third chorus practice when her instructor had to stop mid-song to reprimand the three friends in the back row. Arturs was always trying to capture the attention of the row of girls in front of him. In truth he was usually successful. His sense of humor, confidence, and charm were a winning combination. He also had the most captivating crystal blue eyes. His voice was powerful, and she had watched several church plays in which he'd played the lead. She snuck a quick glance in his direction, and his eyes caught hers. His ever so slight nod of appreciation colored her cheeks with embarrassment. This is how Elza and Arturs first met.

Chapter 7

Arturs' family: his father, Voldemars, mother, Berta, older sister, Helena, and youngest sister, Anna, lived on a large piece of land outside the town. It was named Veckisi. It had five buildings on it and a house on the hill. The view from his house was the best in all of Gulbene. Arturs' family had owned the land on both sides of the main road for many generations. As you walked up the entrance toward his house there were rows of "Liepas" trees along each side. They came together at the top to create a canopy of amber colored flowers that smelled like honey. Elza said she especially loved the horse and wagon rides in the winter. These trees made a snow covered tunnel they would go under to get to the main road. In the darkness, covered in big blankets, you could hear the jingle of the bells around the horse's neck. In the summer the tall oak trees would surround a beautiful rose garden in front of the house. There was a tall shade tree to the right of the porch and an apple orchard behind the house.

Near the stream in the back of the property, as the story goes, your great, great, great grandfather buried cubes of gold in a metal box when he came home from Russia at the end of World War I.

"Really!" my grandson exclaimed, "Where is the buried treasure now?" Nobody knew where the spot was, and although many family members searched, it was never found. I saw sudden disappointment in both my grandchildren's eyes. Clearly this had been the most interesting part of the story so far!

Inside his house there was a large kitchen. It had a wood burning stove with a high brick chimney. Behind that was a formal dining room with a long table and long benches on each side. There were two bedrooms. Below one of the bedroom windows was the "root cellar." This was where they stored all the vegetables. It was dark and deep, and when the sirens sounded during the war times, the family would run and hide there to be safe from the bombs.

The Nogobods family was known for having the sweetest beets in Gulbene. Back then you didn't have a grocery store. Everyone would leave fruits and vegetables near the street and you and your neighbors would go by and choose what they needed! Everyone wanted Arturs family's beets.

Arturs' family photo, from left; Berta, Helena, Arturs, age 12, Voldemars, Anna in white dress.

Elza's confirmation picture, age 13

Chapter 8

Elza's best friend, Alise, could not believe the change she saw in her. Alise was the outgoing one. She had long legs and shoulder length dark hair, but her green eyes were what everyone envied.

Alise was always encouraging her dear friend to participate in more of the school outings. Elza was shy and felt more at home on her family's farm. When Elza's eyes looked as if they held a secret, Alise was very excited to hear about Arturs. Arturs apparently was the reason for the continuous smile that showed off Elza's dimples.

Alise, as it turned out, had been dating Arturs' favorite cousin, Fritz Jaunzemis. Fritz was a tall blonde with dark eyes who was known in Gulbene as the one who was always eager to help out his friends and neighbors.

The two couples got along beautifully. Many church dances and holiday gatherings would find the four friends laughing and dancing together. Both girls had fallen in love. They spent many nights up late talking about their experiences.

Elza and Arturs spent much of their spare time together during the next few years. They usually would go with a picnic of fruits and fresh breads to the park. The park was filled with wooden tables and many rose gardens. The aroma was a feast for the senses. A dozen trees meandered around the wooden tables. Across the street was where the train would stop. From their table you could see the excited faces of men and women waiting for their family members and friends. Everyone had beautiful bouquets of long stemmed flowers in their arms. It was the Latvian tradition to greet everyone upon arrival with arms filled with colors and scents! She said it was exciting to sit and talk with Arturs while watching the families uniting. You could feel the excitement build as the train's whistle sounded announcing the arrival of loved ones. It never got old. Children ran and played in the park while their parents stretched necks to see the first glimpse of the incoming train. It was such a wonderfully peaceful spot.

During one of their picnics, Arturs told Elza that when he was younger he spent his free time helping his father plant apple trees, berry bushes, and fruit and vegetable gardens. He told her that early one morning his father, Voldemars, had said he would need help planting a sapling near the front of the house. His family had trees of several shapes and sizes there for years, but needed a tree near the front porch. He hoped it would grow to give shade to an area with many uses, such as a favorite spot to peel freshly picked vegetables, apples, or to take off shoes meant only for the barns or fields. It would also be a great place to simply visit with friends or family away from the hot kitchen in the summertime. He told her that sitting there, listening to the breeze whistling through the birch trees, was Arturs' father's favorite way to relax. His father told him this would be a most special tree. This tree was being planted for a reason. He said he'd told him the hole in the rocky earth must be very deep. The soil, used for their vegetables mixed with various home grown fertilizers, would be placed in the hole. Small rocks would be mixed in for drainage. He said his father took extra care in showing him just how important each step was to enable the tree to form good, strong roots. "The secret to strength and the ability to survive all it must weather, were in the roots," he'd told him. It was a beautiful early spring morning, and they had been enjoying their time together. When the dirt had been padded down and the last bucket of water had soaked around the base, they sat on the porch admiring their work. The tree was about six feet tall with ten or twelve branches. His father had told him he would need to water and fertilize it. "I've taught you well, make me proud" his father had said.

Your great, great grandfather had been a very strong man. He would get up every morning hours before daybreak. He was the first one in the fields and the last one to come in well after dark. Arturs' older sister, Helena, had gone to school and was a school teacher. She was married to a principal named Rudolphs. They lived in Latvia near the Russian border with their three children, Guntis, Maija, and Ievina. The distance kept their time together during the year minimal. His younger sister, Anna, was his mom's helper, and he was the only son. They were very close. Living with his mother, grandmother, and sister made their relationship even closer. He and his father were the only males other than hired help. His family had owned their land for over 100 years!

Arturs' father found much joy in taking the grain to be made into flour on Saturdays. It took two hours, round trip. In the spring he especially loved it. The spring flowers beginning to sprout up were a sure sign that the long, cold winter was over. Sometimes he would let Arturs ride with him. He told me those were special times with his father. They could watch the seasons changing from their seats up on top of the wagon. Their horse always knew the way and looked as if she had enjoyed these weekly ventures as well.

One Saturday morning Arturs' father decided to take his young filly instead of their six year old mare. The mare had cut her leg, and it had not yet healed. Besides, he thought the filly was ready to earn her keep. Arturs begged him to take him along, but he was experimenting with the filly. Voldemars was eager to see if the mare could pull the weight of the wagon. It would be quite a lot of extra weight with the bags of flour piled high. He told Arturs to help in the fields instead.

Arturs was not happy. Some of their best conversations took place on the way home. The roads were pitted from the winter snowfall, but they were dry. The morning ride there must have been especially beautiful. The warmer weather had painted the hills with flowers of every color. It was a sunny day and his father surely was proud of their young filly along the way.

Voldemars had picked up the flour and had been on his way back. He was about twenty minutes from home, approaching the top of a hill, when the accident had happened. In fact I was told you could always pick out their property from the top of that hill. On a clear spring morning, from this view, you could count the help in the fields. He had been so close.

Arturs was helping in the fields when his mother came running for help. She was very young and at this moment looked like a child, helpless, confused, and frantic. He'd never seen her like this! The neighbor who had owned the farm where Arturs' dad was found had just given his mother the grim news. He had said he heard an engine and turned to see if it was a motor car. They were just beginning to see motor cars in the nearby towns. The farmers in Gulbene were not happy about the noise and dust they kicked up. The neighbor said he saw Voldemars' young filly get spooked by the approaching car and rear up. Somehow the reins had wrapped around the wheel of the wagon and also around his father's wrist. The young filly picked up speed. His father, sitting on top of the burlap bags filled with flour, lost his balance. The filly, unaware, continued to gallop. The neighbor said he ran as quickly as he could to help him. He couldn't see him at first because he had fallen on the far side of the wagon. But as he came closer, he saw the driver of the motor car kneeling over him. He was very upset trying to communicate what had caused the accident. Apparently Voldemars had been dragged by his horse, entangled in the reins, several kilometers down the road. His neck had been broken. In an instant such a strong, warm, hardworking man with a young family, was gone.

Arturs had to be strong to be the only male in the household. At fifteen he had to quit school and take care of his family, a responsibility he took very seriously.

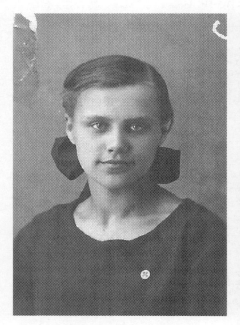

Elza, age 13

Siblings: Anna, Arturs, age 20, and Helena sitting in a chair.

Chapter 9

It was a sunny spring day in early March when Arturs asked Elza to marry him. Elza was 19, and Arturs was 24 at the time. They had been sitting on the small bridge that led to the church. It was a beautiful white church with a very tall steeple. Many times they had stopped during their walks at this very place. The water from the small brook under the bridge tumbled over the rocks and glistened in the afternoon sun. The peaceful sound of the water trickling through the rocks was the perfect backdrop for their many conversations. They had been courting each other for the past seven years.

They were married on April 21, 1930. Alise and Fritz were their best man and maid of honor. They watched with Arturs as Elza walked down the aisle. Elza wore a wedding gown that she had made herself. She had a long veil made of tulle that was held together with a wreath of fresh flowers on top of her head. Her curly light brown hair and blue/green eyes looked especially beautiful! Elza was carrying long stemmed white lilies. Arturs said he'd never seen her look more beautiful. He was a very lucky man! Now their bands of gold would unite them forever. They were very eager to begin their married life together on Arturs' homestead.

Arturs and Elza's Wedding Photo

Arturs and Elza's Certificate of Marriage

Elza lived with Arturs' mother, Berta, and his younger sister, Anna. She told me she would work alongside the help in the fields. It was here, in the fields three years after her wedding day, that she went into labor with her first child. A beautiful baby girl they named Kitija came into their lives on September 24, 1933. Five years later, on June 7, 1938, they were blessed with another daughter. Her name would be Inara. Their little family was growing, and life at Veckisi was peaceful.

Arturs and Elza enjoyed being parents. Elza dressed their daughters in beautiful dresses that she would make.

On Sundays the girls would also have their hair gathered in large bows. Many friends would comment on how beautiful their family was. Arturs was very proud of his family. He so enjoyed being a father. He often would be the one to tease and play with his girls on Sunday afternoons after church. Kitija enjoyed helping her mother and grandmother, while Inara loved to be in the barns with her father. They knew very little in the beginning of the strife they were about to experience.

Latvia had been occupied many times in the past. The port outside of Riga was sought after in many battles. However, in 1939, Hitler and Stalin signed the Molotov Pact, which was publicly known as the Non-Aggression pact. It stated that Germany and the Soviet Union would remain neutral if attacked by a third party. The secret part of the pact, however, included the division of northern and Eastern Europe into German and Soviet spheres of influence. As part of this secret pact, the Soviets annexed Estonia, Latvia, and Lithuania. Around this same time, Latvian officials met with Lithuanian and Estonian officials in a public meeting. Together they formed and published the magazine, "Revue Baltica." This was a literary and cultural publication. The Soviets, however, accused the three Baltic states of holding a secret meeting and instead publishing an anti- Soviet magazine. Latvia, not knowing all that was involved in creating the Molotov Pact, tried to stay neutral.

On October 2, 1939, the Soviets tried to take advantage of its rights under the pact. They demanded Latvia allow 30,000 troops on their land. The reason they were given was fear of Nazi occupation. This was a lie, of course. It had been planned the whole time. The Latvian army, although proud, was small. The government thought they would be destroyed if they resisted. They reluctantly agreed. Soviets camped out on the west side of the Venta River. In November that same year, Estonia and Lithuania also agreed out of fear, and an unlimited number of troops were placed on their soil as well.

On June 14, 1940 the Soviets overran a Latvian guard post on the Russian front. On June 17, tanks surrounded the Riga airport. All broadcasts were interrupted and placed under Soviet control. President Ulmanis attempted to calm the Latvian people using a mega-phone in the streets. He was deported and on June 20, the Latvian National Government ceased to exist. The new government proclaimed Latvia a Soviet Socialist Republic. By July all property was confiscated and all farmland was nationalized.

Living under Soviet occupation was far worse than they ever could have imagined. After all properties were nationalized, each Latvian family was given a Russian family to share their home with. Borees, Vera, and Viktor came to live with Arturs and Elza's family. Borees was a Russian soldier. He was gone all day and late into the evening. He talked little and when he did, there were no other conversations. Clearly the line had been drawn. They were there to care for his family, and their home was now his.

Chapter 10

Vera, Borees' wife, was hostile towards Elza and degrading to Berta. Arturs and Elza now shared a bedroom with his mother, and both girls. This was uncomfortable for the entire family. Berta's dream was to be able to see Riga just once! She had spent her entire life so far in Gulbene. Under Soviet occupation her dreams looked dismal. She told Elza, "Well, it looks like I will never see Riga in my lifetime."

Living in such small quarters with the Russians left little opportunity to have conversations without eager ears. To do so they would go to the park near the railway station. The roses were gone. The trees were still there, but their branches did not provide shade from the sun as much as they provided shadows. In this shadowed area Arturs and Elza could come and talk quietly with each other about the disturbing situation. It had become increasingly difficult to have Borees' family living in their house. They treated his family like slaves in their own home. They hoped the occupation would end soon, and life would get back to normal. Arturs would become the man of the household again and retrieve what was left of his dignity. Arturs and Elza's first priority was the safety of the girls. It was here that Elza told Arturs about the bruises that Kitija had been coming home with. Kitija had told her about the walks to school with Victor. He was nine. Kitija, at only seven years old, was being hit and kicked on the way home. It was not uncommon to have the Russian kids pushing around the Latvian children. Their children had never experienced anything like this, and were vulnerable. The Russian kids took advantage of this. Arturs was visibly upset. He was a proud man. He had been with the "Aitsargos", The Defenders of Latvia, much like our National Guard. Now he felt his hands were tied. In every instance, he had to swallow his pride for the safety of his family.

He would talk to Kitija when she got back from her studies that day. He told Elza there had been talk of Latvian families on a list. This list supposedly was made up of Latvians who could cause trouble for the new Soviet government. Arturs' sister, Anna, was married now to a wonderful man named Arnolds. They lived nearby. Anna and Arnolds were trying to get more information from friends and family to see if there was any truth to this list. Raimonds, his friend and neighbor, was equally worried. Elza's mother and father still lived in her childhood home. Her father obeyed and did as he was told. It had been eight months since the start of the Soviet occupation and he still had his home to himself. That was not to say he was not watched. In the beginning, the family would meet at his home. Information had taken time to arrive. They were all living under the watchful eyes of the Russian families who had invaded their households. It was difficult to tell which was truth and which was rumor.

Chapter 11

Elza was always complimented on how she could create beautiful clothing from simple pieces of material scraps. Easter of 1941 was no exception. The Russian family who had taken over their household had moved into the city. Borees was apparently needed in another area. The sun shone a bit brighter this particular Easter. The trees all had traces of green on their many branches. The hardship of the long, harsh winter months was coming to an end.

Everything looked glorious as they climbed onto their "Sunday wagon" and headed down the canopied dirt road. The Liepas trees were in full bloom and the aroma was spectacular. What a joyous morning to be celebrating the resurrection of our Lord! The girls, Kitija and Inara, looked like angels with their curls tied in beautiful white ribbons. Their dresses swung around their legs as they ran to greet their friends in the church yard. Arturs had longed for a son, as all farmers did, to take some of the burden off his shoulders. However, as Elza glanced his way, the pride in which he watched his beautiful girls frolic was undeniable.

Church had been filled with songs sung by a new generation of choir boys and girls. There had been greetings by friends and family alike. Arturs however had walked outside with Arnolds and Fritz. By the disturbed look on his face, Elza knew it must be more dreaded news. Alise and Elza exchanged worried looks. The Germans had been bombing the countryside. Although they would rather be under German control than Russian, the fighting had begun to get increasingly closer to Gulbene.

The day that had started out so bright had become overcast. When they arrived home from church, Berta had prepared a feast for their family and friends. Anna and Arnolds helped set up the table, that was always placed under an apple tree in the backyard. The first row of the apple orchard was a beautiful backdrop to all family celebrations. There were pink roses in a bucket in the middle of the table. Elza's mother Jule, and father, Peters, had just arrived with baked goods that you could smell clear across the table. Arturs popped a pirag in his mouth as he turned to greet Fritz and Alise. Their daughters, Margita and Vijia skipped up the drive, each holding beautiful bouquets of purple and yellow tulips. Fritz's sister, Rita, and their stepbrother, Konrads, made quite an entrance with a fully cooked goose! Even Helena and Rudolph's family made the long trip. Helena was pregnant and lived quite a distance away. It was truly a treat to have everyone together! Kitija and Inara ran to greet their friends and cousins. Elza's brothers were all married by now, and their children walked up with colorful baskets of goodies.

They started their Easter tradition of taking turns with the "Easter Egg War" contest. They always made the eggs the night before Easter. They used onion peels, carefully wrapped them in cloth, tied them tightly with string, and boiled them. Each egg was unique, with shades of browns and gold. On Easter everyone at the table would choose an egg they thought stronger than the others. At this time, the fun would begin. The idea was to hit the challenger's egg at the top or bottom. If yours stayed strong, you moved onto the next competitor. Inara was always the first to lose, as Kitija vigorously hit her egg and gleamed with delight. Arturs always showed such anticipation towards the egg event as he was always the ultimate winner. We think he cheated, but would never admit to it. This Easter, however, he seemed preoccupied. He went through the motions, but there was no sparkle in his eyes. Once the table was cleared the girls ran with their cousins down to the water to unearth "special stones".

My grandson's sleepy eyes were looking up at me. "I want to look for special stones too, Nonnie!"

"Maybe at the beach tomorrow," I told him. "We have rocks there shaped like hearts!" But before I could make a plan, his eyes closed. I snuggled him closer as my granddaughter looked elated to have my full attention!

"You're not going to stop telling the story about your Nana are you?" she asked eagerly. I gave her a big smile as I continued.

Elza asked Arturs what it was that he, Fritz, and Arnolds had been talking about. They had taken a walk along the stream bordering their property. Taking care to not let their discussion be overheard, he explained that the German front was getting increasingly closer to their homestead. They were making a strong push to take Latvia from the Soviets. It had been in the Soviets' hands for almost a year now. Their lives had been awful. They were constantly living on the edge never knowing what the next dawn would bring. Arturs said he'd like to take the girls down to Volfrids homestead for the night. It was only 20 minutes down the main road. The bomb shelter he'd dug had proved itself as a safe haven when the Soviets had first invaded their quiet little town.

Elza's heart sank. She just didn't understand when this would all end. Even on these days of memory-making, they could not enjoy peace. She looked out the window to see the girls chasing each other, hands filled with blue forget-me-nots. How innocent they were. They didn't know of the crumbling world around them.

It had been sunset as they gathered the girls and Berta and made their way to Volfrids' home. They told the girls it would be a fun filled night with their uncle. He and his wife did not have children of their own and loved to spend time playing with both girls. They had their night clothes with them and were very excited! Elza's brother would not take them into the shelter with their grandmother, unless it was necessary. He, in fact, thought Arturs and Arnolds were alarmed without reason. Not having a family of his own gave him room for error with the ability to find safety in a moment's notice. Arturs did not have such a privilege.

They walked into Volfrids' home just as the sun set. He had a pile of wheat just waiting for Kitija and Inara. He knew how they delighted in making jewelry from the strong, pliable stalks. The girls ran in excited! After talking about a plan with her brother, should there be trouble, they walked in the darkness back to their home. It was eerily quiet. The horses in the coral seemed agitated. As they approached the cleared path to their house, they saw the first flare cut through the evening sky. Their hearts pounding, Arturs directed Elza to get to the house. Arturs began running to take the horses into the barn. However he had only gotten a few steps ahead of her when the bombing started. The roar overhead was deafening. The Germans were bombing their hometown, trying to make their objectives quite clear.

They ran to the root cellar. It was along the side of the house underneath a large oak tree. Arturs took the wooden cover off quickly, and they lowered themselves into the damp darkness. They huddled together amid the new harvest of beets, potatoes, carrots, and onions. The darkness engulfed them, making them invisible to both their enemy and each other. Elza began searching the pocket of her dress to find the worn paper that held a written prayer. It was kept safely in a tiny pouch she had made. This prayer had become part of her everyday dressing routine. It was a prayer that started as far back as the 1500s. It was supposed to keep you safe; it gave her comfort just knowing it was with her. She clutched it, knowing it by heart, and began reciting it silently.

The squeal of flares piercing the evening sky above was alarming. The Soviets were sending them up to find their targets. Their dogs, Liska and Retz, were barking incessantly. They covered their heads as a natural reflex. There were countless explosions in the not too far distance, more screeching, and planes roaring overhead. Panic welled up in Elza's chest as she pleaded with God to keep her girls safe. Shivers crept up her spine. Then all at once there was the most deafening explosion to the east of their house.

Thirty more minutes passed before the sky began to quiet, Elza mentally prepared for what they would find. They heard crackling and the most horrific sounds from their horses! Arturs, eyes wide with fear, slowly lifted the top off the root cellar to peer out. The most frightening groan escaped from his very core. Elza crept up to see two of their buildings, the pig stall and the cattle barn, both in flames. They ran to see if the fires could be controlled, but the third building, the building with the horse stalls, had caught fire also. A flare had most likely landed on the cattle barn igniting it and spread quickly to the other two. Their dogs ran to them, looking equally terrified.

Tears streaming down their faces, they listened to the heartbreaking sounds of many of their panicked pigs, cows, and horses. There was nothing they could do but watch. The heat from the inferno kept them from getting close enough to make any difference. All three buildings with much of their livestock had perished. Luckily, two of their horses had been in the coral. They were frightened but safe. Their house on the hill was far enough from the flames. They would not lose their home this night.

Through the smoke coming up the drive to their house was their neighbor, Raimonds. As he came up the road, he saw the flames, and he said his heart sank. He feared he had lost his friends and closest neighbors. He told them that he had spoken to Volfrids. Berta and the girls were scared but safe.

The bombing took place nearly every other night for the next several weeks. Each night they took the girls and Berta to Volfrids. These were very tense weeks. The loss of livestock was secondary to the fear of losing their family to the war. The girls cried every time they left them at their uncle's house in the evening. Arturs felt they would be safer in Volfrids' shelter at night. The raids were always at night. Elza and Arturs ran to the root cellar every time the sirens sounded. During the daytime they spent most of these weeks cleaning up from the fire. Daily chores and their daily routines in general had come to a stop. The Germans were moving ever closer to defeating the Soviets. The surrounding towns and parts of Gulbene had many areas marred by bombs. The beautiful country hills near their home looked foreign. The colors the flowers had always painted across these nearby hills were gone. They were replaced instead with fear. Fear of the unknown.

Prayer written in the 1500s. Elza kept it in
her pocket at all times to stay safe.

Nana's Prayer (English interpretation)

I am the Father, Son, and Holy Spirit. I will help all who believe in my word. Keep this prayer with you always. I, the Father, to whom you rely, will save you from all evil threats. With my strength I will keep you safe. My angels will watch over you in all your journeys. He who trusts in my word, I will save and grant a long, and blessed life.

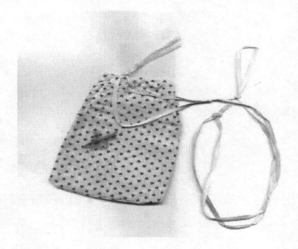

Pouch Elza made to hold her prayer

Chapter 12

There was a new tangible fear creeping into their hearts. Arturs had been hearing rumors but wanted to see for himself. He went down to the park next to the railway, hiding this time with Fritz and Arnolds in a heavily wooded area to the south of the park. They crept closer quietly, knowing that if caught, they would no longer be able to protect their families. What they witnessed was more horrific than all the rumors combined. There were hundreds of people. Latvian people. In all likeliness, many people they all knew. Women, men, children, and elderly people all being herded onto freight trains meant for cattle.

They apparently were taken from their homes as they were found. Children without shoes, infants in only a diaper. They were pushed, slapped, and dragged by Russian soldiers. What was worse were the sounds of children's cries that filled the stagnant air. Parents were yelling for children who had been separated in the frenzy. Fathers' attempts to stand up to the soldiers were silenced by the butt of their guns. They were pushed onto train cars without windows with standing room only and one bucket in the corner for human waste. The rumors were true: the Soviets were gathering up Latvians by the hundreds. Supposedly their names had been on lists. Lists composed by the Soviet government. They were arresting people that they thought would not be good for the new Soviet Republic. They were men from the Latvian army, former policemen, judges, teachers, doctors, and students. Anyone who Moscow perceived to be a threat. They were arresting them with their families, giving their property to the Russians, and taking them to concentration camps deep into the woods in Siberia.

The three men left to get back to their families as quickly as they could, each going through a mental list of why they possibly would be on those lists. After talking with friends and family alike, they decided to gather together and come up with a plan in case they needed to leave quickly. They would meet in Volfrids' barn the next evening. Tonight it was already too late, as the sirens had begun to warn families to take cover.

The next day, June 14, 1941, was spent trying to get as much information as they could. Elza found out a distant cousin of hers had given Arturs' name to the Russian authorities and told them, "This family isn't good for the new government because Arturs had been in the Aitsargos." Suddenly, the worst of their fears had become a reality. Elza and Arturs spoke with Anna and Arnolds and the rest of the family. They needed to start packing and leave. It was about 5:30 pm, and everyone was frantic gathering up what they thought important to bring. Elza was doing her best not to frighten the girls by telling them instead that they were going to stay in a neighboring town with some of their aunts and uncles. They wouldn't have to be separated at night anymore. Kitija, and Inara, thought this sounded like a holiday.

Liska and Retz began barking, trying to alert them. The brown pickup truck, driven by a Russian soldier, was creating a cloud of gray dust as they turned towards the homestead. Elza gathered the girls with Berta and hid in the bedroom. Not knowing why two Russian soldiers would be walking up to their home, a sixth sense, knotting up her stomach, told her that this was how the families were being taken to the railway station to be deported to Siberia. She sat with the girls on the floor of the bedroom with Inara on her lap and Kitija and Berta on each side. Her hands began to shake. Trying to hide them, she slipped them into the pocket of her apron. There she felt for her prayer. She hushed the girls and closed her eyes.

Within minutes she heard Arturs quieting the dogs and speaking to the soldiers. Her heart beating so loudly in her head prevented her from hearing what was being said just a few yards away. Arturs closed the door and soon motioned for them to come out of the bedroom. Inara ran to one of the windows that looked out to the front of their property. Elza chased after her and caught a glimpse of the truck with families huddled together in the crowded truck bed. Inara, recognizing one of the children from a neighboring farm, began to cry. She was upset because she didn't get to have a "ride in the truck!" Elza was grief stricken. The cries from the children would never leave her mind or the faces of neighbors that they each had known all their lives. Fear was etched across their faces. They were all families just like her family, trying to survive in a war that was not theirs.

Arturs looked ashen. He told Elza that they indeed had come to take them to the cattle train. They had asked how many were living here. Having heard six, they said they would need to unload and return. They apparently had started loading families into the truck from the farthest farms from the town first. Arturs and Elza's farm was the second farm from last. Raimonds was the closest. They simply had run out of room in the truck.

Their minds reeling, they began making calls to see who had already been picked up. Jule and Peters, Elza's brothers' families, Helena's family, and Arnolds and Anna were all accounted for. Arturs tried to hide the fear in his voice as he told Elza that Fritz and Alise were not answering their phone. After checking with their extended family, he became even more concerned. No one had heard from them. Berta began to cry. She loved her niece, Alise, and was especially close to her family. They prayed they would hear from them soon and that relief would follow.

Arturs and Elza began collecting food and clothing. They felt sure the soldiers must be coming back at any time now to continue what they had started. It was difficult to shield the girls from the obvious upset on their parent's faces. Berta kept her emotions hidden while helping Kitija and Inara pack. The plan was to leave just before dawn.

The phone rang and Elza answered it. "Oh, you are still there!" was all that was said in Russian before the phone went dead. The truck would return.

Chapter 13

Elza and Arturs had been up for several hours organizing their escape and hoping they would have time to leave before the truck came back for their family. Just after midnight the sirens sounded. Everyone crowded into the root cellar, exhausted both physically and emotionally. Inara began screaming because she had left her blankie in the bed. No words of comfort or reprimanding would quiet this child with the stubborn streak. Surely she would give up their hiding place with her wailing. Arturs gave a quick glance to Elza and then quickly took off through the darkness. He bolted down the steps a few minutes later, much to Inara's relief, with blanket in hand. It would be here in the dark dampness that they would listen to the battle both in air and on land until nearly dawn. When they allowed themselves to climb out to absorb what had taken place, they were elated. The Germans had pushed the Soviets back, occupying many of the towns including Gulbene. The Nogobods family would be spared from going to the Siberian camps. Just twelve hours had divided their fate.

After the Russians had attacked Finland and occupied the Baltics in June of 1940, Hitler felt threatened by the way the Russians were acting on their "territorial ambitions." In response, German tanks reached the Latvian frontier on June 15. By July 7, 1941, all of Latvia was in German hands. However, by invading the Soviets, Germany had broken the secret Molotov pact.

Not everyone had been as lucky as Arturs' family. Information initially was difficult to come by. Families were trying to connect with each other. Arturs was visibly shaken as he told Elza about Alise, Fritz and their two beautiful daughters, Vijia and Margita. Alise, eight months pregnant by then, had traveled three hours into Riga to the hospital to have a doctor treat twelve year old Vijia. She had a middle ear infection. When she was released from the hospital, Alise thought it best to have Vijia stay nearby the hospital with friends. This way she could be close enough to go back for treatments. The rest of her family traveled home to Gulbene. After almost a week, Vijia was still unable to reach her parents. The friends she had been staying with were also worried. They took Vijia back to her house only to find out that her mom, dad and sister had been forced out of their home to be put on the train to Siberia! She had collapsed devastated in sorrow onto the floor of her home.

It wasn't until a few days after arriving home that she had found out her mom, Alise, had faked labor pains to avoid getting on the train. She knew if she got on she would never see Vijia again! Her sister, Margita, latched onto her mother's skirt and snuck away with her mom. A kind stranger took her and Margita to the hospital in his car.

Vijia was reunited with Alise and Margita in the hospital. She was very sick with blood poisoning and had not had the baby yet. Arturs' voice broke when he told Berta and Elza that Fritz, along with his sister, Rita, had been forced onto the train to the camp in Siberia.

Elza, Berta, and Arturs wept as Arturs continued with the details of the separation between Alise and Fritz. The heartbreaking details were unimaginable.

Sixteen-thousand Latvians were arrested and loaded into cattle cars and sent to Siberia on June 14, 1941. Fritz Jaunzemis had been taken to a camp deep into the woods in Siberia. He wasn't given much food and was slowly starving. His sister, Rita, in the same camp would hide bread and sneak it to him when she could. Rita chopped wood eight hours a day for eight years. She was then sent to another camp for several more years. Eventually she made it out to live in Canada with family. Fritz, however, would not get to meet his newborn son, Jekabs. He was born just two weeks after Fritz was forced onto the train. He never saw his family again. He was shot and killed near the end of his first year in Siberia. He was only thirty two.

Latvian leaders immediately began reforming their government, hoping the Germans would restore their country's independence. Unfortunately, this would not happen. The Germans took over their government. Latvia couldn't have their own military force. Many Latvian Jews, gypsies, and mental health patients living in institutions, were all exterminated. The Gestapo also had Latvian Nationalists deported to concentration camps in Poland and Germany. There wasn't an open conflict with regular German troops thankfully, because they shared a common goal: to destroy the Soviet Union.

The rest of that summer was filled with families trying to find some resemblance of normalcy. So many families had been ripped apart. Elza and Arturs stayed in close contact with Alise. The girls would spend the day together while their dear friend cared for Jekabs. There was no communication with friends and families who had been taken away. Gulbene was a very small town, made smaller by the evacuation of innocent people. The friends who remained took care of the grieving families, welcoming them into their own. Slowly a new normal was achieved.

Inara and Kitija were oblivious to the monstrosity that had taken place. They were so happy to be back in their own beds and delighted to play in the summer sunshine. They spent their days near their mom and papa as they worked on the farm. They played in haystacks while Elza and Arturs cut the hay and stacked it so it would dry for feed. They also used it to stuff their sacks where they slept. They both loved having their sacks fluffed up with extra hay. The hay stacks made perfect little houses also to play in. They could spend the afternoons, using their imagination. Elza watched them with obvious delight.

Sometimes they would help their dad collect branches, wood, and small rocks to use to heat the sauna. The girls loved to throw water from the creek on them and watch the steam erupt! It was especially nice in the fall when the days were beginning to cool down. Elza would help Inara bathe in the stream at the back of their property. Kitija would collect tiny purple flowers near the edge of the stream and with a little water, rub her hands together. The lather they would make would be used to wash. The water was always so cold. To warm up they would run to the sauna. These were happy times.

Soon it was too cold to bathe outdoors. Winter was fast approaching. With it though, would bring Arturs' favorite holiday of the year: Christmas! Arturs would bring Inara, with him to find the perfect Christmas tree. They would go across the road to their property used for grazing. There were many evergreen trees lining the northern side. Arturs would always have one picked out months before Christmas. But Inara, quickly becoming the tomboy of the two girls, enjoyed immensely going with her papa to pick out the perfect tree. He always made her think she indeed had chosen it herself. It was his secret. She would carry a couple of small branches that had been trimmed near the base to give to her mother for decorating. Her papa would drag the freshly cut evergreen through the newly fallen snow. The tree, once in place in the small sitting room, would fill the entire house with the scent of pine, "the scent of Christmas!" Kitija and Elza would hang homemade hand crocheted decorations, in many colors. Then they would clip small candles to the ends of the longest branches. On Christmas Eve, everyone would sit down to a feast of food. This was the night everyone would look forward to. The entire extended family would get together with close friends to celebrate. The festive table with red and white wildflower arrangements held delicious assortments of flavorful dishes from their farm. After dinner, everyone would go into the sitting room. Papa would light the candles and lead everyone in singing "Silent Night". The warmth of togetherness on this special night would be felt throughout the year.

Chapter 14

Shortly after the New Year's celebrations, Volfrids became ill, and his wife was very worried. He had been to the city several times with complaints that included lack of energy and yellowing of his eyes. The doctors were trying medication, but his strength was not improving. He was rapidly losing weight. One day in late spring, he was trying to entertain his young nieces. They loved him so. He was making small crosses for the girls' little pet cemetery at the very end of the vegetable garden. The ground had finally thawed, and the tiny crosses made of twigs could be wedged into the earth. Each one marked a special place where a furry friend could be visited and remembered.

Kitija made it into the small kitchen first. She was out of breath and wide eyed! "Uncle Volfrids was lying down near the garden!" she told her grandmother. Berta quickly called Arturs to take him to the hospital. But Elza's oldest brother, Volfrids, would not make the three hour trip to Riga in time. His liver had simply stopped functioning.

During the funeral service, Kitija and Inara each placed two small crosses on his grave. They cried quietly, not fully believing they would not see their favorite uncle again. Elza, walking away with both arms draped around each daughter's shoulders, could hardly keep her own tears in check. Volfrids had always been there for her. He had kept her girls safe when she could not. He'd been a good friend to Arturs and a wonderful big brother to her. Jule and Peters walked away as if in a dream, not able to completely make sense of their loss.

On June 7, 1942, Inara had a festive fourth birthday celebration. Alise came over with her daughters, Vijia and Margita, and little son, Jekabs, now nearly a year old. The swing was hung from a large oak in the yard. She enjoyed having the attention on what turned out to be a very warm June day. Inara opened a gift from her papa, a beautiful doll in a yellow dress. It was her first doll, and it had been her mother's doll when she was only two years old. She had come to Palmati with it. Oh, how Inara would love this special gift! Everyone gave her a beautifully wrapped gift, but it was her mother, Elza, who gave her the best gift of all! She would be having a brother or sister right after the coming Christmas! Everyone was so excited and hugged her mother. It would be a very long seven months!

There were undertones of unrest. The Germans appeared to know something was on the horizon. Rumors were ever so slowly starting to surface. The Fall came and went without any changes. Winter was especially cold that year. Jule had started a cough just after Christmas. Elza, eight months pregnant by now, would go over to help her mother. They would bake together and prepare meals. Elza was hopeful the new medicine would help her regain some strength. Her mother was very much like Elza. Kind hearted and beautiful, they were strong women. Jule always valued time she could spend with her only daughter, the baby of her family. However, as the winter days trudged on, Jule continued to get even weaker. She was very frustrated that she could not help her daughter who was so close to giving birth to her third child. Elza had always been a blessing to Jule, who could not wait to meet her new grandchild!

The morning of January 8, 1943, Jule did not wake up. She had slipped away in her sleep while her daughter was in labor. Elza was in labor throughout that morning and into the evening. No one told her about her mother. Not long after midnight, a beautiful little girl was born. Her name would be Olita. She was healthy and strong. She had beautiful eyes, and little wisps of hair. Arturs and Elza were in love all over again. Olita filled a place in their hearts that they didn't know was empty. Kitija and Inara were very excited to have this little sister. A real live doll!

Elza was devastated to find out about her mother! How could such a joyous day be clouded with such despair? She sobbed. She sobbed because her mother would never meet her precious granddaughter. She would never see those beautiful eyes that looked so much like hers! Mostly she wept because her mother would be buried that day, and having just delivered her baby, she would never be able to say goodbye.

Little Olita gave life to the Nogobods family. She was such a sweet child. She slipped right into her family's life giving everyone happiness in the most simplest of ways. A smile from this little one could wipe away the sadness in her grandfather's eyes. She would ease her father's tired back, after a long cold day working the farm, with a warm snuggle on his shoulder. Berta helped Elza care for her, and Kitija and Inara spent every spare minute playing with her. It was Elza however, who felt the blessing of this little life the most. Little Olita helped keep the tears back when she missed her mother. She also added excitement to the long, dark winter days.

Chapter 15

It was in February that Hitler signed the order to create the Latvian Legion. He then drafted, in accordance with this order, 148,000 Latvians. They would be ready to fight the Russians should there be a need to. The Russians kept warning of an attack. The Germans would be ready.

Spring brought much rain, and by June everyone was happy to feel the sunshine on their faces. Peters spent much of his time with Elza and Arturs on their farm. Elza tried to give him small chores to uplift his heart. She couldn't help but feel the sadness that engulfed him since Jule had passed away. Olita, now able to sit and play with him, gave him a temporary refuge from his loneliness.

The next year was filled with laughter. The holidays were joyous. Olita was constant entertainment! It was so refreshing to have a little one around. Once she began walking after her first birthday in January of 1944, there was so much for her sisters to show her. She loved the barns with all the tiny chicks. Her giggle was infectious! Kitija taught her how to take the raspberries off their bushes and place one on the tip of each finger. Then eat them one by one! Inara taught her that the big tub where Papa used beets to make homemade beer, had lots of bubbles. Lots of bubbles to play with! The froth was very sweet. Inara scooped some off to sneak a taste sometimes, much to Kitija's astonishment!

Elza's 34th birthday on July 2, 1944 was not met with the usual festivities. Hitler had the Latvian Legion posted in Eastern Latvia. Should the Russians make a move he would be there to meet them. He would keep the Latvians on the front lines to absorb the most casualties. They would be the first ones to explore the hidden mine fields and take on the opposition's fire. They had no choice. July 3 brought the dreaded confirmation. The Russians had moved into Latvia early that evening. It was time for the family to come up quickly with a plan. Elza woke up all three girls who could not possibly know this would be the very last time in their warm beds. The Nogobods family, the Jaunzemis family (including Konrads, Alise, Vijia, Margita, and Jekobs), Anna and Arnolds Pommers and Helena and Peters all met in Raimonds' barn. Vilhelms was very ill at the time and couldn't attend. Arvids and his large family chose not to attend because he, his wife, and five children would have no other choice than to stay in Gulbene. He thought it would be impossible to travel and feed his five children. In the barn, the kids were all put back to sleep on blankets on the hay. Arturs and Arnolds were organizing a plan to leave the next evening. They thought it would be wise to travel at night and get to one of the towns to the north. This would give them some distance away from the Russian front. Everyone was in agreement except Peters; he didn't feel he would be strong enough for such an escape. He also was confidant the Germans would make a strong stand and keep them safe. Elza pleaded with her father to come with them. Her heart was breaking! She could not bear to leave him behind! The next town could be traveled to within two or three days. He would be able to stay on the wagon, and they would stop when needed. It scared her to think of packing up her daughters. Olita was only 16 months old; Inara had just turned 6; and Kitija was 10. But staying, so close to the front, was not an option in her mind. Her father would need to think it over and change his mind.

As they sat in the dimly lit barn, they could hear the bombing in the distance. The kids were waking up and asking to go home to their beds. Berta lay down with them to keep them calm while the families made plans. They decided that there would be 41 wagons in all and they would meet outside of Gulbene just after dark the next evening. They would travel in a caravan and be able to help each other.

The sun was beginning to peak through the cracks in the barn door. It was decided then. They would all go back and begin packing. They would need to have a week's worth of food and water available for their horses and livestock. They would each take two horses and two buggies. They would also keep their plan to themselves.

After Berta had made a big breakfast for everyone, the packing began. Elza ate nothing. Her stomach was in knots. What to take? What to leave? Olita was playing on her blanket at Elza's feet. The innocence of the moment in comparison with what lay ahead was too much. She tried to hide her tears, and Arturs came over and gave her a reassuring hug. He told her it would only be for a few weeks, a month at most. They would come home and have a belated birthday for her!

Kitija and Inara were frightened. They hadn't slept much in the barn and had been scared listening to the families talk about the bombs, about what would happen if they stayed, and about leaving their homes to stay someplace else. Who would feed the new down covered baby chicks? What about Liska and Retz?

Arturs was on the phone with his sister, Helena. She also believed they were leaving without proof of an impending attack and that her brother's "hunch" was not supported by much of the extended family. She would talk with him tonight before they left. She had agreed to take care of the house and do her best with the property and animals. Peters also, would not change his mind and he would be checking on the farm. Arturs loaded the flatbed wagon and piled it high with blankets and clothing. There were boxes loaded with smoked hams, cooked chickens, turkeys, dark rye bread, butter, cheese, apples, and potatoes. They heard bombing again in the distance. It was unusual to hear it during the afternoon. German planes were flying overhead. There was an uneasy feeling in the barn. Even the animals could sense the tension. The roar overhead did not help. The bombing came increasingly closer. Arturs decided he would take the two gray horses as they were strong and dependable. He'd had them for five years now. One would pull the "Sunday" wagon and the other would pull the flatbed wagon.

Chapter 16

There had been a stream of German trucks on the dirt road in front of their homestead. Anxiety had filled the air. It was late afternoon when a truck loaded with German soldiers turned into their property. Arturs met the fear in their eyes with his own. They would need to leave their property! The front was closing in on them. The German soldiers needed the hill that Arturs' family had called home for over three generations. They needed to dig trenches to battle the approaching Russian troops.

Arturs made a quick call to Arnolds to alert him, and then he rushed to gather his family. Elza held on tight to Olita as she ran with her crying toddler to climb up onto the Sunday wagon. Inara and Kitija, both frightened, ran with Berta to the wagon. After tying two cows to the flatbed wagon, and a colt to the other wagon, Arturs ran to the barn. His family sat high on top of the wagons while the German trucks, filled with many soldiers, rushed down their beautiful driveway. The air previously filled minutes before with sweet scents of honey and jasmine, now smelled of fuel.

The small frightened family sat and watched while Arturs ran to free all the animals. Horses, cows, turkeys all ran in confusion. Arturs hoped beyond hope that they might have a chance at survival. Arturs led the way sitting upon the Sunday wagon. He hurriedly pulled down the driveway. The German soldiers pulled their trucks to the side, allowing room for them to get down their entrance. There was no time to second guess, the soldiers directed them to where they could meet up with the German army. The gray mares galloped under the canopy and onto the road that divided their property. Arturs heart was in his throat as he watched Liska and Retz dutifully following alongside him. They were part of his family. They had watched over his family for more than ten years now. They had been loyal up to their last moment. He yelled for them to go home! Tears streamed down his face, knowing he would never see them again. At first they didn't listen, and tried to follow their family, but eventually they could no longer keep up. First Retz sat down and then Liska. Within minutes Arturs could no longer see them in the screen of dust.

Less than 30 minutes had passed before they had reached the top of the hill. Everyone looked back in horror. Their house was ablaze! In fact all the buildings were on fire! The Germans soldiers had wasted no time before clearing their homestead in order to dig their trenches. There were no comforting words that would dull his family's heartache. No preparation could have lessened the magnitude of this pain. Their home and everything they had just left behind was gone. Arturs and Elza's generation would be the last family to have lived at Veckisi.

Numb with sadness, they continued to the rendezvous point. Arnolds and Anna were waiting for them. A few families who had met in the barn had not made it, including Raimonds and his family. The Jaunzemis family, including Alise, three children, and Konrads however, had made it. There were 41 wagons that had begun this journey to flee from the Russians. Arturs, only 39 years old, could not have imagined the journey he was about to embark on. They were told to stay with the retreating German front and that the German soldiers would keep them safe.

Chapter 17

Some of The Latvian Legion soldiers fought alongside the retreating German Soldiers. Most were on the frontline. 300,000 Latvians left most of their property. 50,000 escaped over land through Lithuania and Poland. 5,000 were able to get onto small ships and boats to Sweden. 160,000 traveled in slow moving horse and wagon caravans that if lucky, eventually made it to German troop ships. The Germans took the Latvians to Germany because they needed strong laborers. All escape routes were attacked by Russian Naval and Air assaults.

Their caravan of 40 wagons intertwined quickly with other fleeing Latvians and the retreating army. Because of this, however, they were easy targets for the Russian air attacks. Their first 48 hours was nightmarish. There was no time to rest at all. They needed to create some distance between them and the Russian soldiers. They were being bombed relentlessly. When the roar of the Russian airplanes could be heard in the distance, everyone would take shelter where they could. Many times their only choice was the mounds of hay in the fields next to the country road. No one talked about home, or their journey ahead. Elza's head was filled with heartache for her father and brothers. They hadn't had time to change their minds. They were not at the rendezvous point with the other relatives.

Arturs was her strength. He appeared strong and in control. However, she alone could detect the anger in his blue eyes. It had been a week now, but what this small family had witnessed, would last a lifetime. There were other caravans with families and friends like theirs, eating from their bundles they had packed, sleeping in barns when they could no longer stay awake, and getting back onto the country roads after only a few hours rest. They needed to keep up with the soldiers, who were both a curse and a godsend. The Russians were bombing the route they were traveling, trying to reduce the number of fleeing German soldiers. Yet without them they would fall into the hands of the Russian front not too far behind.

The family had traveled well beyond the town north of Gulbene where they had expected to wait out the struggle. Nowhere in Elza's mind had she ever anticipated this. Her home and everything in it was gone. She was traveling with her baby, two young daughters, her husband, and mother-in-law. The bombing was relentless. They had divided the family in groups of two. One adult was with each child. Arturs went with Kitija, Berta with Inara, and Elza with Olita. When the bombings would start, each would run for shelter of any kind. The planes dropped bombs on the roads trying to halt the advance of German soldiers. More than once their caravan had crossed over bridges minutes before they were bombed. The families travelling behind them were killed and the families on the other side, left as easy prey for approaching Russian Army.

It was difficult to know which explosion was from the Russian bombers or from the Germans retaliation. There was death everywhere. The fear never left. If they survived the latest attack, their relief lasted only minutes. Once they regrouped onto the wagons, they would travel past the horror of families not as fortunate. They saw a grieving woman leaning against a dead horse. Her despair was deeply felt by all who passed. They saw families grieving near dead family members, the surviving members had given up the fight, not caring to live in a world without the lost loved ones. Many survivors walked alone with nothing, having lost everything. The caravans continued this way, teetering between life and death.

Four weeks passed. This time when they stopped to rest, the German soldiers had given them hope. The soldiers were hearing bits and pieces of encouraging news. The Russian advance was slowing down. They were bombing the roads less frequently. Miraculously, the entire group who they had left Gulbene with was still together and healthy. This tiny bit of hope had given energy to Elza and Arturs. They found a place in a roadside barn to sleep. Elza was talking to Anna when a passerby remarked how beautiful her daughters' eyes were! "Three small diamonds in the rough!" Such a simple statement, yet Elza felt proud. These three girls were her pride and joy! That night she reached into her pocket to find her tattered paper with her prayer on it. As she recited the prayer, she thanked God for her precious daughters. They were truly the reason she found strength to move forward each day. To get them to a place where they would be safe and happy once again was her only mission. She slept better that night than she had at any time previously along this journey.

It was nearing the end of August. They had started the day traveling with an impending storm. By noon there were claps of thunder, and lightning that zipped through the overcast sky. The rain was cold, and the dirt roads were covered with deep, muddy ruts from the horses and wagons. The poor gray mares, having had little to eat, were very thin. They were slipping as they lost their footing in the mud.

It wasn't long before the family heard the rumble of the fighter planes fast approaching! This time they were met by the German air assault. Elza ran and took cover with Olita in one of the hay piles. Arturs and Kitija scrambled to do the same. Berta began running with Inara but slipped and pulled them both down into the mud. The last thing Elza saw was Berta getting up and holding Inara's hand, pulling her towards a hay pile on the opposite side of the road. Suddenly, the sky lit up, followed by a deafening explosion. The Germans had hit one of the Russian fighter planes. The fiery debris from the doomed aircraft began raining down all around the family. The haystacks they took refuge in were no match for this warfare. Unfortunately all they did was create a visual barrier from the battle around them. The ground was in flames. Elza, trying to calm Olita, peered out. The sight she saw terrified her! The field across the road was littered with large parts of metal in flames. The haystack where Berta and Inara had run toward was gone. Lost under the mangled mess. All she could see was thick black smoke and flames! Panic set in as she ran towards the smoke carrying her frightened child. Her worst nightmare crept into her heart. She fell to her knees unable to get any closer. Sobbing, she saw Arturs running towards her with Kitija, fear and confusion etched across his face. It seemed like an eternity before she saw the muddy silhouettes coming towards her through the smoke- filled air. Berta and Inara had run to another haystack. They were upset but safe. Everyone was equally muddied after the reunion. No one cared, for their little family had once again escaped disaster.

At this point in their journey, most of their food was gone. They had been traveling for two months now. Elza did what she could to replenish their supplies. She would collect berries from the bushes along the way. The girls enjoyed this also. They helped get vegetables from the abandoned gardens and water from the wells.

Chapter 18

It was early September. The good news traveled fast in the long procession of wagons. The Germans were holding their front. Finally the families could stop and rest for more than a few hours. They came to a large town in northern Latvia called Cesis. The plan was for everyone to split up and find work and a place to stay. Arturs and Elza found work on a farm. The Latvian family offered to let them stay in a very large building with all their extended family. They worked in the fields and, in turn, were given food and shelter.

The early fall weather was beautiful! The trees were covered in oranges, reds, and yellows. Everyone was elated to be off the road and enjoying their family and friends again. Berta watched Olita during the day. Both Kitija and Inara helped on the farm. They milked their cows, fed their chickens and pigs. They especially liked the little baby chicks! Everyone enjoyed this small respite for a couple of months. At the beginning of November, with the bitter cold of winter just around the corner, the Russians once again broke through the German front. Arturs bitterly gathered all the wagons again and loaded them with food and supplies. They had learned during their stay that German ships were bringing in more soldiers and supplies to the port of Liepaja. They were in turn taking back refugees to Germany. It would take about a month to travel to the port. The family they had been staying with, begged Elza to leave Olita and Berta with them! They also offered their thirteen year old son to travel along with them, thinking he could be of some help. They believed Berta, the oldest and Olita, not yet two, would not survive the cold winter journey.

Elza said "No, we survive together or we die together."

The caravan had the same families traveling in it as the previous one. Yet it looked and felt different. The group was suffering through the bombings yet again, but their fear of not surviving in the cold very much heightened the harsh reality of their situation. They were no longer trying to wait out the "struggle" and return to their home towns. Now they were trying to get out of their beloved country. The future looked even more dismal.

The winds picked up along the long country roads as Fall was winding its way towards Winter. Everyone looked defeated. It had been two weeks of cool fall days and increasingly colder nights. Many children and adults alike were getting sick along the way. Elza was scared to think where this journey would take them. The fear was worse than any hunger pain. It took all her energy to stay positive for her sweet little girls.

Arturs trudged on with his jaw set. He kept his head high and refused to give in to the hopelessness that was invading an ever-growing number of hearts. He knew he had the strength to get through whatever lay ahead. He would take one obstacle at a time.

The caravan reached Riga on its way to the port in Kurzene-Liepaja. In an ironic twist of fate, Berta's dream of seeing the capital of the country she loved was bittersweet. The cobblestone streets were filled with German tanks. The quaint outdoor cafés she had heard about were now only memories under the piles of rubble. The beautiful architecture, however, still stood tall. The city, the largest in the Baltics, had been marred, but not destroyed, by its invaders. The intricately sculptured faces atop the ornate buildings seemed to watch over their caravan. The golden roosters adorning all the churches defiantly pierced the blue sky. Berta especially had longed to see this. She told the girls that the rooster, according to Christian tradition, was a vigilant defender against evil. Its morning song could drive away bad things. This symbol, during their final farewell to the country they loved, gave them renewed strength.

The caravan completed their journey to the Liepaja port one week later. It was a welcome sight to see the ships unloading soldiers and equipment. They had made it!

Chapter 19

Elza, the girls, and Berta, boarded the ship ahead of Arturs. Elza kept a close eye on him from the deck of the ship. She knew how hard it would be for him to leave their gray mares that had courageously marched across this war ravaged country. She could feel his heartache as he was told he had to leave everything. He had to choose one thing to bring onto the ship. How to choose? He glanced over the belongings. They were all he had left from his home in Gulbene. Defiantly, he grabbed his pillow and climbed the stairs to join his family. So it was from this deck, aboard the Lapland, that they watched their homeland gradually drop out of sight. Each of them quiet, their heads filled with hope of a return, and fear of the unknown.

They arrived a week later in Germany. Everyone was shuffled into huge rooms, while German authorities tried to find someplace to send them. After three weeks in Gotenhafen, they were shown a list of German families who needed help in exchange for food and shelter. The entire group of family and friends continued once again to travel together. They headed toward areas that had been on the list. They were excited to be far from the front and free to live as they pleased. They found a beautiful lake in the small town of Veren Morich and decided to regroup there. The weather was wonderful. The beginning of December proved to be cold but full of sunny skies. They slept in homes that were abandoned. They enjoyed each other's company at night and started to look at their work options. There were castles nearby that they had been told needed help on their properties. Arturs and family found work here for Baron Smith. The others also found work in nearby castles, just in time for the full onset of the winter of 1945.

Arturs and Elza worked on the property. Kitija and Inara attended German schools alongside German students. Berta took care of fixing the meals and taking care of Olita, now two years old. They were all very hard workers, and Baron Smith appreciated this. He paid them wages and gave them food and shelter. They were all so thankful to have a place to stay, hoping the front would hold through the winter. On the weekends Kitija and Inara worked beside Elza. They would go early into the grand castle and complete housekeeping duties. They all appreciated such an opportunity to not only work inside during the winter months, but to be among such fine furnishings and linens. Kitija dreamt of how it must feel to sleep in one of these grand beds. The walls were covered with portraits and paintings, canvases filled with so many beautiful colors. The painting of a flower garden invited the eye to follow the paths leading up to a magnificent church with a tall brick bell tower. Kitija told Elza she would someday be married in just such a magical place. Elza glanced at her oldest daughter. She was just twelve years old, with beautiful wavy dark blond hair. Her eyes were big and her smile was contagious. She looked a lot like Elza when she first met Arturs. Kitija was her biggest helper and a very hard worker. She was shy like her mother, but possessed internal strength and integrity like her father.

Inara was a curious one. At seven, her bouncing blond curls and blue-green eyes gave her the resemblance of an angel. However ten minutes with this little rebel, and one would have known that she kept Elza on her toes! She would prefer to work in the fields with her father than around so many breakable, untouchables. She did not like constantly being reprimanded by her older sister and mother, to stop touching the Baron Smith's valuables. So when Elza found a jeweled bracelet in Inara's pocket one evening, she was exasperated but not surprised. It was her father who was beside himself! He tried to explain how improper it was to take something that was not hers and how much it could effect the future of her entire family. The Baron and his family had treated them so well. The repercussions of such an act could lead to their dismissal! Inara immediately felt awful for making her mother and father upset. She said that since the Baron's family had so many bracelets, she thought it would be ok to just take one. Arturs breathed a sigh of relief when Elza had placed it back in the Baron's bedroom the following morning. Apparently it had not been missed. However, as soon as spring had arrived Inara was in the fields with her father more often than inside the walls of the castle.

It was May 1, when they heard they all must leave again. The Russian front was closing in. The Baron gave Arturs and Elza one week's pay, and left them a wagon and two oxen. Baron Smith fled with his family and the only horses. Arturs piled their food and blankets high onto the old wagon. Once again they met with the other family members.

Chapter 20

The first day, while traveling with the German army, it was obvious to everyone that they would not be able to keep up. The German soldiers were constantly yelling for them to move faster! But they no longer had horses. The oxen were too slow. They were falling behind. The Russians were gaining on them and everyone was tired and on edge. Elza tried to comfort Olita, who had begun a habit of shaking her fist in the air when she saw a plane coming! There was no way for her to understand what was happening, but if a plane came over she always had to run...this much she knew.

With the dawn of the third day, it was over. The German army was no longer in sight. The Russian army had been gaining on their caravan all night. There were Russian soldiers coming towards them from the south and also from the west. Within an hour of daybreak, they had sandwiched them in. Their long courageous march to freedom had come to an end.

Elza was terrified. She knew these ruthless soldiers had no consciences. She began to tremble. Tears were streaming down Berta's cheeks. The girls huddled next to their mother horrified. Arturs felt helpless against this powerful surge of evil. The soldiers walked up to each of them demanding money, jewelry, and all valuables. Arturs handed them his week's wages. Then the soldier grabbed his wrist and yanked off his father's watch. Bitter hatred became seeded in the depths of Arturs' heart. This moment would stay with him until his last breath.

The families were forcibly corralled within the Russian soldier's tracks. The front that closed them in had at least 500 plus soldiers. The men who attempted to take a stand were shot. The others, about 200 men, women and children, did as they were told. They were guarded as prisoners of war. The soldiers would come at night to rape the women. Elza disguised herself as best she could. She knew if she looked old, they would move on. Apparently she accomplished this quite well, for on the second night one Russian soldier looked at her and remarked to another, "This one is too old to have these youngster girls," and laughed as they continued on to the next group. Arturs knew how to speak and understand Russian well and he understood their conversation. He however would keep this knowledge to himself.

They trudged along for a few more days before stopping in a small village in Eastern Germany that had been abandoned. The Russians took over the village. It was very close to where the English and Russian zones met. On May 8, news of the German Forces surrendering after Adolf Hitler committed suicide meant that World War ll was officially over. Amazingly, all of their family and friends who had left from Gulbene, were alive and still together. There was overwhelming relief at this news that spread throughout the village! Finally the bombings would end. Although they were under Russian control, they were elated that they were all alive and safe.

The Russians sent them to work in a nearby castle in Neheim, Germany. Arturs and Arnolds' families began working on the grounds. All the children began going to German schools. It was June, the summer of 1945. The war was over. They were not sure what the Russians' plans were for them. There was talk of sending them back to Latvia. The rumors however were frightening! They were hearing that living under Russian occupation in Latvia would mean having curfews, travel restrictions, and race laws. The government had taken away farms from the Latvians who had decided to stay and they had resorted to using the black market to feed their families. Violence had become a way of life for the Latvians. This was not the homeland they wanted to go back to.

Shortly after being taken to this German village, Kitija began feeling weak. She had had a dry cough for about a week and was complaining to Elza that her stomach had been hurting. She was barely eating anything and felt hot and sweaty. Both Elza and Arturs were very concerned. They kept her from attending the school in the village hoping that a bit of rest would give her strength. By the middle of the second week, her stomach was extremely distended and she had lost a lot of weight. She continued to feel feverish. Elza took her to the makeshift hospital in the middle of the village. They diagnosed her with typhoid fever. The doctors said that many young people had the same unfortunate diagnosis. Many along the journey had drunk unknowingly from contaminated water. They would house her at the medical facility and hope for the best.

Elza stayed with Kitija the first few nights, helping to bring her fever down as best she could. The Russian staff said if Elza was not able to pay for her treatment, she would need to leave to make room for the other ill patients. Many like Kitija had been traveling across several countries in less than healthy conditions and were waiting for health care. Many lost their lives in the wait.

One morning as Elza approached the building where Kitija was being cared for, her legs became weak. Her frail twelve year old was lying on a cot of straw on the front porch. She had a gray cover over her. Her skin color was nearly the same as her sheet. She lay there without motion, her eyes half open in what had been known as the "typhoid state".

Frantic, Elza approached the doctor. She demanded to know why her daughter had been put on the porch! (Knowing full well this was where they placed the gravely ill patients.) The doctor explained that her daughter was in very poor health and the hospital didn't have enough antibiotics to meet the needs of an overwhelming amount of ill patients. They needed to choose the patients with the best chance of survival. Elza quickly ran back to Kitija to let her know she would be feeling better soon. There was no acknowledgement. Only a faraway stare and mumbling. She was becoming delirious! Elza knew she needed to find a way quickly to give her oldest daughter a fighting chance.

Arturs wasn't back from his day of work. Inara, however, would be helpful. Arturs would never have let Elza go to the black market, let alone bring their seven year old daughter with her. He was a man of great integrity. He always respected the law. Elza, however, in her heart of hearts knew she must do something. Her family came first, everything else was second. Inara had gone to the black market with her before to get food and clothing. She was curious but she always stayed close to her mother. This time they collected as many cigarette butts as they possibly could. Knowing that of all items to trade, cigarettes were in high demand. After a few hours they collected enough cigarettes to trade for a piece of dried ham. Elza was elated! She was confidant she would be able to trade the ham for antibiotics and care within the hospital walls.

That evening she returned with Arturs to bring the ham and pray that it would be enough to start the antibiotics Kitija desperately needed. Arturs began to cry as he walked up the steps to find his first born asleep. He could not wake her. She had lost so much weight and she looked incredibly young and frail. How could she have walked across two countries, stopping and going for 12 months without becoming ill? She survived an entire World War, only to succumb to a deadly illness within a week of its ending! This could not happen; Arturs gave a strong nod to Elza and walked into the hospital with the wrapped piece of ham in his hand. The doctor accepted the ham knowing he could trade it himself for cash to buy the needed antibiotics. They both clung to each other, tears running down both their cheeks, as they watched the nurse carry Kitija inside to share a room with another young girl her age. She would begin the medication in the morning.

Elza stayed that evening, making Kitija as comfortable as possible. She still had not opened her eyes. Elza pulled out her prayer from her pocket. It had always given her comfort. As she recited the prayer, she pleaded with God to save her daughter, praying that she had not been too late. She sat near her bed willing her daughter to wake up. Kitija was her biggest little helper, taking care of her sisters, with not so much as a complaint. She was wise beyond her years and had had to grow up too quickly.

The next day as promised Kitija was given her first round of medication. Twenty four hours later she opened her eyes and began drinking small amounts of water. A few days after that, her fever subsided and she began to sit up and eat a bit of soup. The young girl lying on a bed next to her also had typhoid fever. Her name was Karina. She had beautiful dark hair that floated about her pillow. Her mother and brother were with her to help her eat and attend to her needs. They were all from a town outside of Riga called Jurmala. They also had taken the same route to Germany as the others.

Karina was good company for Kitija. Being the same age and having just gone through many of the same experiences, the girls had much to talk about. They both would tire easily. Rolling their eyes at the endless pampering from their mothers, they would comfort each other in middle of the night when neither had their family with them. They promised to keep in touch with each other when they were sent back to their families to finish their recoveries.

It had been two weeks since Kitija had been taken to the hospital. The doctors had told Arturs and Elza that she could finish her recovery at "home". They needed the room for others who had been waiting. Kitija was very weak and unable to stand up or walk. But very eager to leave. Karina had become weaker and her fever was rising. She had not had a conversation with her in three days. It was unbearable to watch her new friend slip away. Arturs carried Kitija back to where they were staying with Arnolds and Anna. The next day Elza told Kitija that she had heard that Karina had died in her sleep. So many awful memories in a year's time. Now Karina. Elza had worried over Kitijas reaction. Elza comforted her, crying softly, knowing just how close she had come to losing her own sweet girl.

Kitija was unable to go to school. She recovered ever so slowly during the next four months, building her strength to nearly what it was before she was sick. Elza once again counted her blessings!

Elza, Olita (18 months),
Inara (7 years old), Kitija (12 years old)

Chapter 21

As Fall approached there was much talk within the family of devising a plan to cross into the English zone. Many of the young people from the camp were sneaking over during the night. They would return before dawn to share what they had seen. The borders were not heavily guarded at this time. It seemed dangerous but not impossible to reach the English camps.

By November, with careful planning the younger couples, from the camp were escaping during the night with fair success. Some were caught and killed. Most were making it. Anna and Arnolds developed a plan to escape. They did not have children, and it would be easier to cross without detection. The rest of their family and friends also were creating plans to regain their freedom. Arturs talked with Arnolds. Both men knew the area well by now. They had both seen the camp just a mile and a half away. They knew the Russian guards' routines and knew what would be the best plan of action. Arnolds and Anna would try it first. If they made it, Elza and Arturs would follow with their family. There were people carrying messages to family members nearly every week now, lending support from the British camps they had found freedom in.

In mid-December, Anna and Arnolds gathered together with the rest of the families with whom they had traveled so far. They announced that they were going to try to make it to the English zone that night. It was a bittersweet moment. Everyone was both excited and frightened for them. If their plan worked, it could pave the way for the remainder of them. No one took this lightly. There were hugs and tears and words of advice. If they made it they would get messages through to them with the young people who had crossed to relay information.

There were emotional farewells, words of wisdom, and promises to celebrate when they were reunited. They had all been together since they had pulled out of Gulbene with all their supplies and their 40 wagons. The wagons and their belongings were left behind long ago. But all the families and friends were still together and stronger as a unit. More than a year later, they were about to separate and not sure they would see each other again. This journey had brought them even closer.

Time came to take the leap, and time was of the essence. The Russians were already beginning to talk about bringing reinforcements to better secure the perimeters. There was also talk of rounding up the Latvians and putting them on trains back to a Russian controlled Latvia. At 1:30 am, Elza, Anna, Arturs and Arnolds hugged, wiped away a few stubborn stray tears, and then they were gone, into the overcast winter night. The wind dipped into the new fallen snow, gently lifting its powder into the air and created the perfect illusion of peaceful camouflage. Arturs and Elza listened carefully, at first to the hurried crunch their footsteps made and then just as quickly, to the silence. The silence was comforting as it did not reveal any hidden obstacles. There was neither shouting nor gunfire cutting through the darkness. Only silence. Arturs decided this was a good sign that his younger sister and his brother-in- law would be successful. It was a difficult night to get any sleep just the same.

Three very long days later they got the welcomed news. Anna and Arnolds had made it safely. Everyone was ecstatic! All the families without children began crossing over during the night. In fact, their entire original group had crossed. More news of success followed. Arturs and Elza began putting together their own plan. It would be much more dangerous with two year old Olita. They could not explain to a young child how to stay quiet while running for a mile and a half in middle of the night in the dead of winter. Unfortunately, they didn't have time to go over options. The Russian soldiers escorted them into a room with many other Latvians. They were told to pack up and be ready to leave on a train back to their homeland. They would all be leaving on December 28. In six days! You would have thought this would be welcome news! The war was over, and they could go back home.

The stories, however, of how missing fathers, mothers, grandparents, children, and babies were found in mass graves were frightening. Many Latvians were also tortured and killed after they were sent to local prisons. There still was the very real threat of being sent to slave labor camps in the Northern wastelands of Russia. Arturs felt that because of his loyalty to his country, his time in the "Aitsargos," (the defenders of Latvia) that there would be no doubt he would be targeted. From everything they'd heard, they would have been escorted off the train in Riga only to be ushered onto a cattle train to the Siberian camps. He and his family had been sought out once, and luckily had been spared. He wasn't about to subject his family to that terror again.

Elza sadly went through the options in her mind. She had heard the rumors also. The risk was too great. She'd been completely cut off from her family since they had left. There was no way to know how her father, brothers or sister-in-law's families were doing? Why Raimonds and his family had not met them that first morning at the designated spot? If they had survived the war? If they were even there anymore. She longed to see her friends, family and in-laws again, but life was cruel. She had finally found a way back to see her family and it was too dangerous. There were too many unknowns with fatal consequences. Reluctantly she agreed with Arturs.

A message had been sent over to Arnolds through a few young men trying to get information for the remaining families wishing to leave. It was Christmas Day when the message from Arnolds arrived. It was the only gift that this Christmas would bring. He and a few people from the British camp would be waiting outside the train station in Berlin. They would have to find a way to get to the pickup truck when they were told to change trains.

Chapter 22

A few days later, on December 28, 1945, having no choice, they climbed up the steps to board the train. The sun was setting as Elza hung onto Olita, not knowing what would be awaiting them before the next sunrise. She had barely eaten anything since getting Arnolds' message on Christmas. Inara was excited to be getting a train ride! Kitija was the only one of the girls to know of the plan to escape. Within minutes everyone had boarded and was seated. It was dirty and cold inside. Arturs chose seats near the front of their train car. He wanted to be close to the Russian soldiers taking them back to Riga.

The sun seemed to be in a hurry to set. It hid beneath the horizon as darkness quickly crept into the train cars. Inara pressed her little nose against the window enjoying the lights speeding by from nearby towns. Olita snuggled up on Elza's lap as the rumbling of the train gliding across the tracks, lulled her to sleep. Kitija and Berta sat side by side not saying a word, the gravity of the situation weighing heavily on their frail shoulders.

Arturs and Elza were alert to every movement, every sound around them. They had a plan. Elza once again softly recited her prayer while holding it in her clenched fist. Later she would describe this dark train ride as "the night from Hell!" The Russian soldiers began walking car to car. This train was meant to force the Latvians out of Germany and bring them back to their country that was now occupied by Russia. The soldiers thought the Latvians would be glad to be going back to their homeland. Arturs planned on playing the part. His acting skills were on par.

The tense quiet in the train was disrupted by angry Russian voices yelling in German. The Russian soldiers had come across two German young men two seats behind Berta and Kitija. They were German soldiers, in civilian clothes, just trying to mix in with the Latvians. Apparently they thought they could make it to Berlin without being found out. The war was over, and through the angry confrontation they could hear the young men trying to explain that they were just trying to get back to their families. You could see the Russians blood beginning to boil as there was a great hatred between these enemies. They commanded the young Germans to get off the train!

Olita was awakened and began to cry. Elza tried to muffle her outburst. She did not want to bring any attention to her little family, her heart pounding loudly. Inara held her hands over her ears, tears spilling out of her big eyes. Kitija closed her eyes as Berta swung her arm around her shoulders. Arturs sat rigid. Eyes forward. The expressionless eyes successfully hid the hatred welling up in his chest.

The soldiers began beating the young men. The young Germans refused to jump out the door of the moving train! The soldiers, undaunted, opened their window and began lifting the men up to shove them through. The German young men fought hard for their lives, but these Russians stood several inches taller and many pounds heavier than the Germans. The screaming ended as their bodies hit the ground. Elza thought she was going to be sick. Everyone tried to hide their disgust, worried that they would be picked next by the evil that controlled their fate.

The Russians continued searching each row on their way to the next train car. Minutes later a shot was heard from the car behind them, and another body tumbled beside the tracks. This continued for what seemed like hours. Arturs and Elza, numb and more determined than ever to get off at the stop in Berlin, resolved to put their plan into action. It began as bits of conversation between Arturs and the two Russians. The soldiers eventually sat at the front of the car on their large duffle bags. From here they could guard the civilians in that car. Arturs knew how to speak Russian well. He had chosen the front seat for just this opportunity.

Their plan started as a conversation between Arturs and Elza, in Russian. They spoke loud enough for the men to hear them and talked about how happy they were to be going "home!" A bit later, Elza noticed the shorter soldier looking up at them as she told Arturs she couldn't wait to see her father. A real tear fell from her eye because in fact she would not be able to see him. She missed him so very much. This conversation had been practiced many times over the past few days. Elza's Russian was not nearly as good as Arturs', but she had practiced this conversation to perfection. Her hands trembled in her pockets but her voice and eyes were steady.

The shorter soldier asked Arturs where he was from. He knew of Gulbene. As the night progressed, the soldiers began to relax and thought it appropriate to pull out a bottle of alcohol. They were drinking, celebrating the end of the war. Arturs had hoped for this. He exchanged comments in perfect Russian, and laughed at their jokes. Soon after they began drinking, what appeared to be Vodka from a bottle, Arturs began to share some of his favorite jokes with them. He had always entertained with ease, and this night was no exception. Somewhere after midnight, they began sharing their Vodka with their new "friend." He pretended to take some to celebrate along with the young soldiers.

The girls had fallen asleep along with Berta. But Elza stayed alert. She did not miss a word of the exchanges. It was hard to watch Arturs laughing, socializing, with the Russian soldiers. Just hours before, they had viciously thrown the Germans out the window! She knew this was all part of the plan; to get the soldiers intoxicated and make them believe that Arturs and Elza's family were very excited to have the war over and to be going back "home." By daybreak, the train whistled to let everyone know that it was approaching the Berlin train station. The Russian soldiers had been drinking most of the night. Elza could tell by the pats on the the backs, the drunken laughter and the relaxed body language that Arturs had indeed accomplished this part of the plan. Elza gathered the girls and tried to keep from trembling. She was terrified as she contemplated the next 15 minutes. There was no room for error. She would get off the train as soon as it stopped and begin walking between the trains as they had been instructed by the soldiers. Each of them would have one of the girls by the hand. In the terminal, they would turn left to get out of the doors to the parking area, praying that Arnolds was able to complete his part of the plan without complication. Timing would be everything. Their family's lives depended on it.

Finally, it was time. The train was slowing to a halt. Arturs gave Elza's hand a tight squeeze and an ever so slight nod of the head. His eyes told her he loved her. They would make it. The soldiers gave their last instructions. They were to stay in a group and they would direct them to where the next train would be waiting.

Elza picked up Olita, still sleepy, and held her tight. Berta held onto Inara's hand and Arturs followed them down the steps holding onto Kitija. Kitija nervously looked up to her father's eyes. He gave a quick squeeze of her hand for encouragement, and then the plan began. Arturs snuck a look over his shoulder to see exactly where the two soldiers were who had been in their train car. They were standing at the steps making sure everyone had gotten off. Quickly, Arturs led the way through the multitude of people. There were many more soldiers standing along the walkway than they had anticipated.

Arturs and his little family walked as one unit, huddled together and trying to mold into the river of immigrants. They could hear instructions being repeated not far behind them. They could see just a few steps ahead where they would need to turn. Luckily there were no soldiers standing at the corner.

Arturs whispered "left" and Elza, Berta and the girls immediately turned as a unit and began walking more urgently within the crowd. Not ten steps into this change in direction, the two Russian soldiers began yelling to Arturs! "This way! The train is over here, my friend!" Arturs yelled his apologies and said he would get his family and turn back. Because of the relationship he had developed with them on the train, the soldiers believed he had unintentionally turned the wrong way. There was no hurry to reach them.

At once, Arturs and his family began running towards the doors. He could only imagine the confusion running through the soldiers' minds as they yelled for them to "STOP!" They ran as fast as adrenalin would allow them to. They could see the parking lot, yet there was much clamoring and confusion behind them. Several other soldiers were also yelling now and their shouts were getting closer. Elza would describe this later as if it had been in slow motion. The exhilaration she felt when she saw the back of the truck, the flap thrown up, Arnolds steady eyes pleading with them to hurry! The gun fire, the bullets intending to find their targets depriving them of the freedom they so desperately sought. The moment when she thought this plan had not been a responsible one for parents to contrive! Their children could die. They could all die! The only sound she remembered were the bullets hitting unintended targets. Her eyes were fixed on freedom! Arnolds scooped up Olita and then lifted Elza into the bed of the truck. The men from the camp grabbed each of the others, and pulled them up in the same manner. Arturs flung himself into the truck with barely a helping hand. The truck wasted no time taking off onto the road while its new cargo rolled and slammed against the truck bed walls. The shots began to fade into the distance, but no one moved from the truck's floor bed.

Gasping for their breath. Crying and hugging. Hearts beating against loved ones' hearts. Relief, ever so slowly, beginning to cautiously replace fear. How can you describe one's first moments of freedom! Twenty minutes later the truck carried the Nogobods family into the English zone of Berlin to a Displaced Persons camp in Hanover. It was December 29, 1945. Arturs exclaimed, "We could finally breathe freely again!"

Chapter 23

Displaced Persons Camps were the responsibility of the United Nations Relief and Rehabilitation Administration, UNRRA. It was founded in 1943 at a meeting of representatives from 44 future U.N. members. It was held in anticipation of likely post-war needs. Billions of dollars were spent between 1945 and 1947, mostly by governments in the U.S.A., Canada and the United Kingdom. Late in 1945, the UNRRA operated 227 camps in Germany, Austria, and France.

The news had spread quickly throughout the camp of the successful rescue. All of Arturs and Elza's family and friends greeted them with tremendous relief. As of that day, everyone who had begun the journey in Gulbene was safe and free! How very blessed they all were! It just so happened that there was a wonderful New Year's Eve celebration planned at the camp.

Elza and Arturs walked up to the celebration as if they were in a dream. The entire family was given clothing and shoes. They had been able to wash and felt a renewal in spirit as well. Elza had fixed the girls' hair, braids with strips of cloth. Her "three little diamonds in the rough" looked especially pretty and were bursting with excitement! Berta even had color in her cheeks! There was music playing as they approached the party. Everyone was dancing! You could hear songs sung loudly and proudly in Latvian! Arturs knew the words and began singing along. Elza slid her hand into his. Arturs swung her around and began dancing.

Berta and the girls watched with full hearts. Elza was instantly aware of why she had been so attracted to this man. He was so light on his feet and she felt as if she were dancing on a cloud! The brightness in his blue eyes returned with every refrain of the songs he'd known since he was a young boy. She couldn't help but smile and the smile, turned into laughter. Before long they were laughing and crying at the same time, all the while continuing to dance. Without breathing a word to each other, they could understand each other's thoughts, and the tears of joy at their great fortune. They were so thankful to have had their lives spared in this war. It had been a long journey, but they had survived together.

To Elza it had felt like a lifetime since they had met in the barn that evening, constructing a plan to leave. No one could have known that it would have led to this night. This night of celebration in a Displaced Persons Camp so far from where they had started. An enormous relief came over them knowing they would no longer have to make the difficult choices in keeping their family safe. The UNRRA would take over this extremely stressful task. They had never felt happier in all their lives. There would never again be a New Year's Eve celebration quite like this one.

They stayed in the camp for four weeks. They were housed in a very large army barracks. They were checked to see if they were healthy enough to move on to another camp. They checked their heads for lice, and everyone had their heads shaved to protect them from getting lice again. They also had many "blasts" removed. These were small, brown, very smelly blood suckers. It was extremely common to pick these up in their travels. Everyone was dehydrated but healthy. Elza was overjoyed! She now prayed every night thanking God for his guidance and the gift of freedom.

Chapter 24

Everyone was happy to leave Hanover and move to the British camp in Melle. They had heard there were many Latvians in that camp. They were hoping to find extended family members and friends alike. On February 1, 1946, they all regrouped and left once again. This camp in Melle was much, much larger than the previous one. The camp had many barrack style buildings but it felt more like a village. Since so many of the people spoke Latvian, it felt like a home away from home.

There were schools already established there, Latvian schools from kindergarten to the university level. This camp was very close to Osnabruck. In Osnabruck, there was a beautiful square. Here dances were held, parties, concerts and sporting events. What a welcome change to the life they had been leading. Upon arrival and after being settled, Elza and Arturs tried desperately to find any information at all about their families who had stayed behind. Konrads, Alise, the girls, and Jekobs were there. Nobody could believe how Jekobs had grown; he looked just like Fritz. There were joyous exchanges and many happy tears.

First came the welcome news that there was a Latvian man named Raimonds from Gulbene in this camp! Raimonds, however, was a very common name. The couple helped Arturs and Elza find the man they were describing. There he was: Arturs' best friend and neighbor sitting at a wooden table eating an apple. Arturs began running as Raimonds began to stand up and recognize his longtime friend. They embraced, no words were said. They simply could not put into words what this moment of happiness had felt like! Both assumed the other had not survived. The reality of what they were seeing, feeling could not be gathered into words. Elza began to cry with them.

Raimonds indeed had tried to make the rendezvous location. He had been too late. He led his family along nearly the same route, and they were able to make it to the port at an earlier date. He had similar hardships, but his family had survived also. Such wonderful news. He shared with them that Helena and Rudolphs had stayed in Latvia and last he'd heard, they and their family had also survived.

Elza's euphoria however did not last long as she found out here that her dear, brave father, Peters, had died. Raimonds said he'd heard that he had passed away from an illness just six months after they had gone. Her ailing brother, Vilhelms, and his family had succumbed to tuberculosis. She sat down quietly next to the wooden table. She did not hear the laughter of the young children hitting empty soup cans with sticks, each one trying to win at a simple game, just behind her. She didn't hear the words of comfort coming from Raimonds nor feel Arturs strong arms placed around her shoulders.

Everything became numb. Not one tear could find its way down her chapped cheek. She could only imagine the softness in her father's eyes the last time she hugged him in the barn. She hoped at the time that he would change his mind and meet them the following day. Her brother and his sweet family were also gone.

And so she would carry this sadness in her heart. The parents who had given her life were gone. She also grieved for her brother and his family. She had not been given the simple, yet so important opportunity, to thank them. To say goodbye.

Camp Melle. Elza far left leaning against a wall in the Displaced Persons Camp.

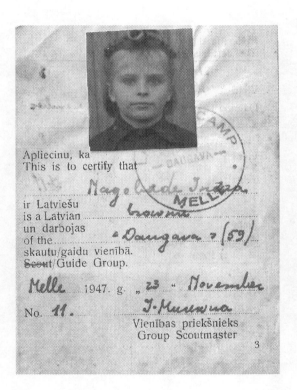

Camp Melle. Inara's camp certification

Inara's school picture in Camp Melle. Standing in back row, second from left.

```
Arturs Nogobods  geb. 30.8.1905. Letland Kreis
                 Madona, Gemeide - Vecgulbene.
1937. - 1944. 29.7. Latvija, Madona Vecgulbene
                    Landwirschaft "Veckišč"
1944. 30.7. Flichtling Latvija, Zenči, Liepaja
1944 2uno 3.11.   mit Schif nach Deutschland
4.11 - 13.11.44.  Gottenhafen. Lager (Lapland)
15.11.44. - 27.11.44.  Meklenburg Waren Müritz
28.11.44 — 1.5.45.        "     Güt Nou Sopsa
                                        Gen.
                                     ub. Kloksin.
        Landwirtschaftlich Weschäftigt.
1.5.45. - 4.5.45.  Flichtling in Deutschland
4.5.45. - 22.12.45.  Meklenburg a.t Alt—
                                    Necheln.
22.12.45 - 29.4.46.  Berlin Zelendorf Linka
15.1946. - 7.6.46.  Hanower Lager Stöcher
                                      Aku
7.6.46. 13.4.48.  Melle, Lager Daugava.
                              c. Osnabrük
14.4.48 - 26.7.48.  Wolterdingen  c. —
                                   Soltav.
26.7.48  30.8.48.  Osnabrück
                         C.M.W.S.
30.8.48 — 28.7.49.  Waldniel  6. M.Gladbach
29.7.49. - 15.6.50.  Min=Gladbach. (Holt.)
15.6.50. - 27.6.50.  Osnabrück.
```

Paperwork documenting where
The Nogobods' Family had traveled and stayed.

Inara, Olita on log and Kitija

Chapter 25

Hours turned into days. Days into weeks. They all lived in very large buildings. They would all sleep on bedding made of straw. Once every so often the bedding would be re-stuffed with more straw. The girls always celebrated this event. Most families had hung large cloths to divide the spaces. Arturs did the same. It gave them a bit of privacy from the others. Their days initially were spent standing in lines to receive food, usually soups from large trash cans, and clothing from trucks. Once a week they would receive an orange. This was the best day of the week. The girls so enjoyed this bright, special, sweet treat. They even scraped and ate the white inside that lined the peels!

Before long the girls began attending make-shift schools. They received an education in all subjects and also learned two more languages, German and English. The UNRRA helped find jobs for all the adults when possible. Elza was delighted to be given the opportunity to teach kindergarten. She loved children, especially the smallest ones. Anna was also delighted to be given a job in the school. Both Arturs and

Arnolds were given work on farms. They enjoyed working in the outdoors. It was familiar and without stress.

One evening in May Anna delighted the family with wonderful news. She was going to have a baby sometime in early December. Just in time for Christmas! It was perfect timing, now that the war was over and they were together again. Everyone was very excited. The girls would have a cousin. They could hardly wait till Christmas.

The time at Melle passed quickly. With the children in school and the adults working, it felt comfortable to have a routine again. On the weekends, they would enjoy festivities and dancing in the square in Osnabruck. It was surrounded by beautiful buildings. The architecture was reminiscent of the tall buildings that surrounded one of the popular squares in Riga. There were many Latvians here. The girls made friends easily, and life at Camp Melle was in some respects, the calm after the storm. It was a cool afternoon on December 8, 1946, when Indulis was welcomed into their world. A beautiful baby boy! He had tufts of brown hair and looked very much like his handsome father. However, when he smiled that crooked little smile and his eyes lit up at the same time…there was no doubt that he'd gotten that from his loving mother!

It was nearing the end of 1946, and the adults had their sights set on getting to Camp Walter Dingen. This was where families awaited clearance. At this camp, families were organized and paperwork was created, to see if they could move to the last camp. This was where sponsors would be found for them. Once sponsors were found, they would be able to leave the camps and start their lives again in a new, free country.

At this point Elza could think of nothing else. Christmas was coming soon, but the days of looking for the perfect tree to decorate, sing and celebrate around, had been almost like a dream. Those days seemed like a lifetime ago. The camp did put up a Christmas tree in between the sleeping quarters. They did their best to decorate and create a festive atmosphere on Christmas Day. Everyone was given a piece of candy on Christmas morning. Olita thought this was the best gift she could ever receive! She had no memory of past Christmastimes. She was so young when they had to leave their home, but Inara and Kitija remembered them well. Christmas morning for them was another sad reminder of what they had lost. Elza and Arturs promised they would once again have their Christmas traditions when they found a new home in a new country.

Christmas was finally here with a baby boy to play with! Many friends and families gathered at night near the Christmas tree and sang Christmas songs. Elza enjoyed hearing all the familiar songs sung in so many different languages. However, she missed the scent of Christmas...pies baking, freshly baked pirags, and a goose on the table with the fresh scent of pine filling every room.

Indulis was spoiled by all. The girls were captivated by him. Olita, now almost four years old, finally had someone to play with. She enjoyed being the "big one" who could finally boss someone around. As he grew, Inara and Kitija took him by the hand and taught him everything. He enjoyed the attention and loved his cousins.

Anna was the proudest mother. At last she could understand what all the fuss was about, and she adored him. However, no one was bursting with pride more than Arnolds for he had a son.

Displaced Person's Camp friends. Inara is the first one on the right.

Inara is the first one on the right.

Chapter 26

One spring day Elza told Anna "each morning it was becoming routine." Before making the short walk to the big gray building serving as the school, Inara, now nine and a half years old, would wake her with her blue ribbon of cloth in hand. It was torn from an old piece of clothing, and if anything was going into those unruly waves of hair, it was always this. The colors were faded, the fabric was worn, yet Inara thought it made the blue in her eyes sparkle. The better to catch the eye of the handsome, dark haired, young man who scooted by on his bicycle every morning.

And so it would go, Elza would pull her fair hair away from her face, tossing it up and winding the shredded blue "ribbon" around and around until it became the perfect bow. A quick smile thrown her way and off she would go. Elza would watch her sit on the large rock just outside their living quarters. She wore her new favorite skirt that she received from the weekly donation truck. It was a light purple. She straightened it around her much too thin legs and began smoothing her hair about her shoulders just so. Just in time as well, because in the near distance, coming up the dry dirt road that bordered their camp, the young man came into view.

His tall silhouette was visible as he pedaled just as fast as he could through the early morning light. He would then slow just enough to allow himself a quick shy glance at her precocious middle daughter. Inara sat there every morning as if she had put forth no effort at all into her appearance, giving the impression that she was able to crawl from beneath her covers looking fresh as a morning glory!

It was at this time, as she watched her daughter hurry to create the perfect memory in the mind of the camp doctor's son, that she saw the transformation taking place. Inara was growing up. Her little tomboy was noticing she could catch the eye of the many boys her age. It wasn't because of her unbridled energy or ability to climb higher and run faster than most of the girls and boys alike. Her appearance was changing. Her little girl was growing up and giving a hint of what she was to become as a young lady.

It tugged at her heart to know that soon she would lose the little one who both frustrated her and fascinated her. Now there would be lazy afternoons of daydreaming with visions of future romances that filled the heads of young girls on the brink of womanhood. Had it really been that long ago when she too had been dreaming of fairy-tail romances while dangling her toes in the coolness of the pond water? She remembered it all too well. Many years had passed since colorful visions of a life yet unseen had filled her youthful heart.

Elza said a prayer for her, for all three of her daughters. She prayed that she would live long enough to see her daughters' dreams become reality. This had become her new prayer, the dream she shared with only her God each night.

Maybe it was because she'd experienced so much fear of loss in the past three years, forever etched in every fiber of her memory, that she'd become so overprotective. Both Kitija and Inara would make the arguments as to why they should be able to learn to ride a bike. Or at least take swimming lessons given by Uncle Arnolds. They "needed" to venture out past the rocky footings at the edge of the large pond near the end of the camp. They wanted to join the other boys and girls who seemed to "float effortlessly," giggling and splashing at the midpoint of the large pond. They argued that they looked childish when they had to stay where the water only splashed about their knees. They also complained that they were the only ones walking along the dirt path, as their school companions rode by triumphantly on bicycles, leaving their eyes stinging with dust and cheeks flushed with embarrassment.

Elza stood her ground even so. Too many of her relatives had been hurt or killed by unexplained mishaps. She'd come too far to let anything happen to these three precious little jewels. So when Inara came in from playing one afternoon and looked quite pale, her eyes rimmed with redness, Elza thought she'd caught a virus. As she told Inara to take some time to rest before their evening rations of soup, she made a mental note. She would take her down to the German doctor who attended to the ill in the camp. She didn't want her damaged immune system depleted any more than it already was. As Inara awoke from her rest to join the family to eat, she looked even paler. She averted her eyes from Elza's concerned glances. She kept her eyes to the floor as if she needed to consider each step with great care. Elza asked if she was feeling a bit stronger to which Inara replied with only a slight nod, never lifting her eyes from the gravel floor. She proceeded to scoot herself up to the bowl of soup and in doing so looked awkward. Elza's alarm began to rise in her chest as she exchanged concerned looks with Arturs. Her rapid breathing was beginning to peak when she watched her daughter stab a piece of potato and wasn't able to reach her eager open mouth! There she sat, stubbornly trying to find a way around her most recent challenge. This predicament, however, would not be conquered with shear willpower. The fear in her eyes began to transform into undeniable guilt. It came in the form of big, salty tears dropping off her set jaw. Elza jumped from the table but not before Arturs could reach her side. He was appalled to see Inara's swollen arm positioned at such an alarming angle. Honesty came in the form of rushed, high pitched sentences, in between loud sobs and anxious breathing. She said she had wanted to learn how to ride Martins' black and silver scooter. He had offered to teach her for many weeks. She had watched him as he mounted it, began pushing with one foot and then with a hop was on his way! He steered effortlessly down the path amongst the boysenberry bushes and white birch trees. It had "looked easy" she confessed. Besides she knew she was more athletic than he. "I had been racing him and winning nearly every time since I turned nine!" she exclaimed, "Surely, I'd be able to follow the simple steps." She expected to accomplish her long awaited feat, but it was not to be.

Martins had held the scooter for her, under the thick covering of bushes so as not to be seen by anyone with the good sense to stop her. However, as she placed a foot on the scooter, it wasn't as steady as she'd imagined. She was feeling quite proud to be balancing and steering until without warning the front tire caught upon a large rock. She tumbled onto a bed of rocks beside a mound of fallen boysenberry branches. She told her mother her elbow hit the rocks and pain began shooting right down to her fingers. Unfortunately the fear of acknowledging her defiance to them proved to be more frightening!

Inara's arm was put in a cast at the camp hospital, while a handsome dark haired boy looked on with guarded concern. No more tears. Elza thought she caught a glimpse of triumph! What to do with a child who looked like a white lily on the outside, but instead was more like a cat of the wilderness in her frail bones!

Camp photo, Inara is on scooter.

Chapter 27

Life at this camp became quite routine after more than a year. Most of Elza and Arturs' family were at this camp. They had friends there, both old and new alike. The girls continued to go to school. They did very well, and Elza was always proud when she walked past one of her daughters, while leading her parade of kindergarteners between the classrooms. Arturs decided to try his luck at singing and acting in the performances held on the weekends in the beautiful square in Osnabruck. He had amazing stage presence and the crowd loved him. Elza, Berta, and the girls loved watching him so relaxed and enjoying himself!

On Friday and Saturday nights there would also be dances for the older teenagers. Kitija was always upset that at fifteen she was just too young to participate! She had caught the eye of several of the boys in camp. She was a beautiful young lady. She had an easy smile, and all the boys enjoyed her company. She dreamt of one day living in a large city. She longed for the city life. She was never a fan of rural living. She always fussed with her beautiful hair and put all sorts of outfits together from the clothing that had been donated to them. She had high cheekbones and perfectly shaped lips. Elza could easily see that the boys would stop at almost nothing to grab her attention. She found it comical to watch as Kitija soaked it all up. Elza was secretly relieved that she was too young yet to be going to the dances in the square. Arturs agreed wholeheartedly! "Time enough" was always his answer to Kitija's complaints.

They were fed the basics and what could be served in great quantities. There were, however, many families in the camps who would take gifts from the Red Cross and trade with the farms nearby for food. Arturs was a very proud man, an honest man. He absolutely would not take part in this. He made his feelings known to Elza and Kitija. They were not to be trading Red Cross gifts in exchange for crops! Berta and Inara, however, snuck to the farms and bartered with Red Cross cigarettes and chocolates they'd been given. They would come home with vegetables and breads. Initially Arturs was very angry, but he too relented after a time when he saw the healthy color ever so slightly returning to his family's cheeks.

By August 8, 1948, they all were given clearance to move to the camp at Walter Dingen. They had been living at Melle for a year and a half. It had become comfortable and their lives had structure. Still, this was what they had been waiting for, their chance to inch ever closer to freedom!

Chapter 28

Walter Dingen was a very large camp. Many of Elza and Arturs' family and friends were also sent here. The paperwork to apply for sponsors began at this camp. It was a lengthy process. By now the International Refugee Organization (I.R.O.) took over the responsibility for the displaced persons camps. They were once again housed, given clothing and food.

The I.R.O. also found work for as many adults as they could. Arturs and Arnolds, having had experience as national guardsmen, were given work guarding several ammunitions warehouses at night. They would leave at the beginning of the week, stay there working every evening, and would return on Saturday mornings. This was hard on everyone, but these were difficult times, and you did what was needed. They made the most out of their time together on the weekends. Indulis and the girls were always happy to wake up on Saturday mornings to meet their papas at the train stop.

The kids continued to go to makeshift schools. Many of the women with experience teaching were given jobs in the schools once again. Berta watched little Indulis while his mama and papa worked. He was getting closer to his second birthday and had boundless energy. Berta was a strong woman, but Indulis used up every bit of her endurance by the time Anna came home from work. Anna also welcomed a needed break when his papa came home for his weekends. They were great pals, and Arnolds was always the proud papa! Frequently carrying Indulis on his shoulders through the camp, Arnolds was as handsome as Indulis was adorable. The sight of this happy duo always brought smiles to the faces of passersby.

Arnolds' November 6 birthday was coming up. He would be working as it fell on a weekday. The plan was to have a surprise celebration the Sunday before. The girls were busy gathering yellow and white flowers to decorate their party table. Their family and friends had brought their food portions to Anna's table. There wasn't much, but at least they could have a nice fellowship with the people who he knew and loved the most.

It was raining hard as Arnolds walked in to find everyone gathered around his table. The dampness of the day could not shake his happiness! The girls all gave him the bouquets of flowers they had worked so long to find and pick. For Arnolds, Indulis' gift was the most treasured! He had gathered his "best rocks" from his special collection and wrapped them in cloth. He was so excited and ran up to his papa leaving a trail of smaller pebbles tumbling behind him. Everyone laughed as he proudly presented his gift to Arnolds. He gave him a big hug as he swung him up onto his shoulders, Indulis' favorite spot, just in time for the Happy Birthday song!

It was just another train ride to work to begin their work week. Arturs and Arnolds were in fact talking about the approaching Christmas Day. They were reliving past Christmas holidays, hoping to be living close enough once the I.R.O. found them sponsors, so that they could enjoy this special time of the year together. The families once again would be eating and sharing laughter around a table filled with homemade desserts. They both had a sweet tooth and missed the way the house smelled Christmas Eve with the wonderful atmosphere, always energized with anticipation!

Arturs had been walking along the south section of the rooftop. This was the building he patrolled every night, five days a week. Arnolds had the next building just a few yards away. No one talked about what was kept inside these warehouses. They had heard they were filled with ammunition. They were heavily guarded. Arturs and Arnolds never asked questions, just did as they were told. From sundown to sunup they were to make sure no one tried to gain access to these warehouses. They always patrolled the rooftops. There were others patrolling the grounds. It was dimly lit, and Arturs could usually make out Arnolds' silhouette as he walked his rooftop.

It was the night after Arnolds' actual birthday. The date had come and gone with the routine of just another workday. It was a moonless night that had followed a cold autumn day. There had been a trace of snow on the ground, but everything had melted before the men got to work. The rooftop, luckily, had been dry when they had arrived. There was just enough wind to give a chill that could be felt through Arturs' heavy uniform. The worst days of winter were just ahead. Arturs wished nothing more than to be living at the camp during the week in Walter Dingen before the dead of winter. He imagined his young brother-in-law across the way felt the same.

Just after four in the morning, there was much commotion on the ground. Arturs senses were immediately heightened. He crouched down, near the edge of the roof, trying to focus his eyes through the darkness. There indeed were two men running. Their silhouettes appeared to be men in guard uniforms. He recognized their hats easily in the darkness. They were running to the east side of the warehouse that Arnolds patrolled. He knew Arnolds would be alert, and would be helpful in whatever they were in a hurry to investigate.

Arturs ran across to get a better look and to maintain the security of his own building. He saw several men; all appearing to be guards, leaning over a pile of cement on the ground. Within minutes there were other silhouettes of uniforms on top of the roof as well. A few were also crouching, and some others were running along the perimeter. Arturs kept low and continued to watch his post.

He was very unnerved by all this action. These nights for nearly four months now had been quiet. There never was more than a car approaching that had everyone on alert. Usually the car was lost and redirected without incident. Stray dogs and chunks of falling snow had the hair raised on the backs of their necks a few times. They had joked that the hardest part of their job was staying awake. This was different. The men on top of the roof were now standing and yelling to the men in uniform on the ground. Arturs heard someone coming up the stairs to the top of his roof. He took his rifle and aimed toward the approaching men. Every fiber of his being was now alert and engaged for whatever was heading his way.

As the door opened, he recognized the voice of Eriks, one of his fellow workers. He was followed by four others. When they saw that the roof top was clear and secured, they approached Arturs. When they explained to him what had caused all the commotion, his legs felt weak. This could not be true! They were mistaken! In the starless sky they couldn't have seen clearly. Surely as they took him across that roof, down those stairs and to the cement pile, he would be relieved. This unfolding nightmare wouldn't have happened.

The brother-in-law who had become his best friend lay twisted amongst the cold jagged cement pieces. A voice that seemed distant told him that another guard had found him like this. He said he must have lost his footing. He was killed instantly. "Lost his footing!" "Found this way!" "Killed Instantly!" Arturs could not, would not, believe this. Arnolds was young, agile, and strong. He had witnessed him survive the impossible during this war. He'd watched him run on the ice and snow to cross into the English zone in the dead of night. He'd watched him pull the wagon wheels from ruts that no one else was able to...this strong, steady young brother of his, could not possibly have slipped. He'd patrolled this warehouse rooftop every night since August. He knew his every step.

Arturs stood up and studied the eyes of every man around him. Surely someone saw something and knew something.

If they did, their eyes gave away nothing. Elza was sleeping, in the dead of the night, when she heard Kitija gasp and sit straight up beside her! Kitija shook as she told Elza her frightening nightmare! She said, "The train had come down the railway, just as it did every Saturday. They were all there waiting for Papa and Uncle Arnolds, but their happy anticipation turned to horror when the large door of the train opened. There was Papa sobbing next to a body on a wooden stretcher covered by an old, soiled blanket." The nightmare had proven to be a reality.

Arturs never went back to that rooftop. He watched his sister crumble as he gave her the horrible news. The stab to his stomach was nothing short of a knife to his gut, as he looked into Indulis' eyes. His sweet little voice asked why his mama was crying. This night, this day, this pain surpassed everything thus far. Their family was forever changed. A little boy, with the face of his handsome father, would never have the opportunity to learn, laugh, and grow with him.

The next day, just one week after his surprise birthday celebration, Arnolds family and friends gathered once again. This time to bury Arnolds. Arturs had tried desperately to find out what possibly could have caused Arnolds fall. If anyone had witnessed his death, they were keeping it to themselves. So beneath an overcast sky, everyone held wreaths of white mums, and one by one laid them to rest with Arnolds. The truth of how he died was buried along with him.

The day finally came, without the anticipated celebration, when they were given clearance to leave Walter Dingen and go to Bedburg Hau. It was December 4, 1949. However, this time all those who had started together, would not be continuing the journey. With heavy hearts, Arturs and Elza put together a small tribute to say a final goodbye to Arnolds. Arturs wept as he said a short prayer and then thanked him, knowing that without his help they could never have come this far.

Arnolds' funeral, Camp Walter Dingen

Chapter 29

Another Christmas…another camp. There was also a tree at this camp, but no one felt like celebrating. Christmas came and went. It was bitter cold here during the winter of 1950. There wasn't much work for the adults, and there was no schooling. The families were going through the lengthy process of placement. Elza was told because she had three girls and a mother-in-law, placement would be even more difficult. The sponsors were looking for young men to possibly help on their farms. Arturs and Elza watched as sponsors were found for other families with able-bodied young men. Their spirits were low upon entering this camp, and now they were very discouraged. Anna, without a husband and a two-year old child, was also a difficult placement.

Finally in March, they all were allowed to go to Dusseldorf. Their spirits were lifted knowing that their paperwork was complete, and they had all passed the required health exams. This camp was where sponsors were sought to take families into their homes. Once they were accepted, they would board a ship and begin their new lives. Where this would be, and the hope of living in the same countries as their extended families, was completely out of their control.

This camp was all business. No one settled in because they could be leaving in a month or two. Families that the IRO had found sponsors for would need to be ready to board the next ship. There were the usual lines for food and clothing. One particular day, when the truck arrived with clothing, Inara spotted an orange colored piece of clothing. She waited patiently in the line and as one item was given to each person, she really hoped she would get that pretty colored piece! She couldn't tell if it was a top or a dress so far back. She told Elza that she was going to ask for it when it was her turn. Elza told her, in no uncertain terms, that she would do nothing of the sort and that she should be thankful for anything they were lucky enough to receive! Elza listened as Inara prayed softly. Inara didn't believe in luck. She closed her eyes and said a quick prayer. After all, she told Elza, "You were always pulling out your prayer, in your pocket, to get what you wanted!"

It took forever in the late spring damp weather to get up to the front of the line. Inara kept praying, making deals with God, "I'll be nicer to Olita. I won't ride any more scooters or steal any more jewelry. I will give Indulis back the rock I took from him to play the world game!" Elza watched her excitement grow and as her turn was approaching she couldn't believe it was still there! "I will pray more!" Inara pleaded!

And then it happened: the nice man smiled at her and reached for the orange dress. Her eyes sparkled with excitement. She told Elza it was the most beautiful dress she had ever seen and it was hers! "The prayers worked!"

she exclaimed with amazement. Elza was delighted to see such happiness in her middle child. After a few minutes, she noticed something else. Inara appeared to be contemplating. Elza asked her if something was wrong? Inara looked at her bright orange dress and then at her feet. She mumbled, "I really like Indulis' rock…"

The summer dragged on and the girls spent time with their new friends. There were animals at this camp, and they were happy to help out with them to pass the time. They took Indulis with them most days. He loved the baby sheep. One afternoon they came back all excited to tell Elza they had watched a baby sheep being born! This had been the highlight of this summer so far.

It was a hot day at the end of July. Elza and Arturs were just about to gather up the girls for dinner. A woman approached them with the news they had been waiting for. They had found Elza and Arturs' family a sponsor in the United States of America! They would be finalizing everything including one last medical check-up and would then leave on the next ship in one week! Arturs grabbed Elza and hugged her tight. They would be going to live in the land of opportunity! In one week! They couldn't run fast enough to tell the girls in the barnyard.

Kitija looked up from the cow she had been milking. How she hated farm life! She looked afraid as Elza and Arturs ran over to her. Inara and Olita saw them also as they entered the barn. They ran to see what was the matter! "We are going to America!" was all they could get out! "We are all going to live in the United States of America!" All the girls began crying and jumping! Everyone was completely elated with this news! Finally, a dream had come true! In middle of the hugging and laughter, Kitija asked, "Where will we be living? Please tell me New York City!" Elza said, "A farmer in Illinois is sponsoring our family. We will be forever thankful to him for giving us this opportunity!" Kitija, at nearly seventeen, began to frown. Elza and the rest of the family could not help themselves, as they burst into laughter.

When they told Berta, she cried. At 69 years of age she was going to experience the best part of her life. All the talk of never getting out of Gulbene in her lifetime, yet here she was still, with so much to see and experience! She looked shocked, hardly believing this was happening to her. How fortunate she was to have survived this journey and to be given the gift of freedom in this great land!

Arturs and Elza hoped that Anna and Indulis would get good news as well. They prayed that they would all be in America.

The next few days were a blur. At night Elza could hardly sleep thinking of the life they were about to start. She imagined plenty of food, a stove to cook with, and cloth to sew beautiful clothes...security. She was too excited to sleep! As she looked around in the darkness of their quarters, she saw that she was not the only one awake with dreams of what was to come. Kitija and Inara were whispering beside each other and giggling about the sights they would see.

Elza looked around her and took it all in. The barren, gray, metal walls of the barracks that they lived in. So many camps, each with the same walls. The walls that had kept them safe in this make-believe world. Walls that kept them from the real world. Life had continued outside of this gray corral for the last four years, while they grew older waiting for theirs to begin again. It was only two days now before they could get on the ship that was coming into the port of Bremerhaven, Germany. They needed to gather all their paperwork and complete one last form. They also needed one final wellness checkup, and the required injections, before entering the USA.

They were up early to get into the line for their health checkups. Inara and Olita were still sleepy and quietly followed their Papa's footsteps. The adults went first, followed by the girls. Kitija was happy to get the shots over with as she was not a fan of needles. Inara took two slow steps toward the lady with the white coat. She took her temp as a matter of routine. When she looked up at Elza after reading it, Elza's stomach tightened. The nurse announced that Inara was running a low grade fever. After further inspection, she saw small red spots on her forearms and hands. They were signs of smallpox. She announced to our group that Inara would need to be quarantined for the next ten days. The rest of the family, however, were healthy and could board the ship tomorrow for the United States.

Olita burst out, "Yay! We get to go for the boat ride tomorrow!" A very disappointed Inara and Elza were shuffled off to the quarantined rooms. Inara had to go, Elza needed to take care of her. Olita tried to understand why this meant they couldn't get on the boat. They weren't sick! Inara's fever continued and she was very tired. The first three days, she slept next to Elza. Elza wasn't sleeping again, now worried about Inara. Smallpox was very serious. The doctor continued not only poking Inara and examining her for more flat, red spots, but also checked Elza continuously. Smallpox was very contagious.

Kitija and her friends would come to her sister's window and visit. They tried to keep her spirits up. They gave Elza updates on what everyone was doing, and then Kitija would bring back updates on her sister to their family and friends. One afternoon, four days into the hospital stay, Arturs brought Olita holding a little baby bunny. Olita held it up to the window so her sister could see how cute it was. Inara smiled, and her spirits were lifted. In turn, her temp that evening was back to normal. Olita credited her bunny visit to saving her sister's life! At seven and a half, this made perfect sense!

Elza did not produce any symptoms that would have been associated with smallpox. By the fifth day, Inara's fever was gone, and the red spots had disappeared. They needed to stay the entire ten days in order to be sure the incubation period was over, and there were no new symptoms. In the end, they had decided Inara never had indeed had smallpox. It was just a virus with a rash.

 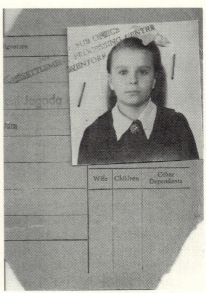

Elza and Inara's camp processing cards

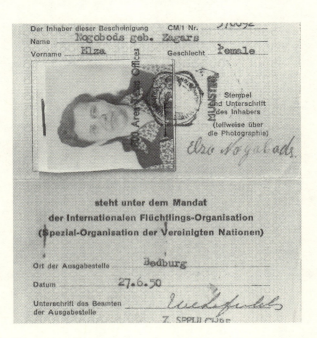

Elza's camp identification card from Bedburg Hau

The Nogobods families
Displaced Persons paperwork

Chapter 30

On August 22, 1950 the Nogobods family had received clearance to travel to the United States. They said goodbye to Anna and Indulis and the rest of their family and friends. It was an emotional farewell, with promises to celebrate once they too had found sponsors. Arturs, Elza, Berta, Kitija, Inara, and Olita all walked proudly up the ramp to board the ship called "The General Hann." It translated to "no frills" but the Nogobods family agreed it was the most beautiful sight they had ever seen!

On August 29th, on the top deck of the ship, Arturs stood tall with arms outstretched to pull his family in close. There it was, the Statue of Liberty. She looked strong and powerful, and a true symbol of freedom without limitation. Their journey had begun six years before when they had been so frightened as they ran to climb up onto their Sunday wagon. The long, hard fought journey had brought them to this moment. Arturs said, "We have fled communism and survived!" Elza looked up to Arturs to see the tears streaming down his face. She kissed his salty cheek. They had made it.

Kitija looked at the enormous buildings creeping ever closer. They seemed to touch the clouds! The morning sun bounced off the glass-sided buildings and sparkled. She had always dreamt of living in New York City, but even in her dreams, it never looked as new and shiny as this! The buildings appeared to be packed together and stretch on forever! Olita cocked her head to one side and said, "America has so many big buildings! How do they fit the farms in between?" Inara giggled at her little sister, "They don't fit them in between! The farms are behind them, silly!" They quickly cleaned their quarters below and lined up to disembark. They stood in line quietly, not understanding all the languages that seemed to be echoing in this building. When it was their turn, the man at the desk asked for their papers. He asked them to give their names and ages: "Berta, 69, Arturs, 44, Elza, 40, Kitija, 16, Inara, 12, and Olita, 7."

Ellis Island. Nogobods photo upon arrival in the United States.
From left; Inara, (12) Arturs, (44) Kitija, (16) Berta, (69) Olita, (7) and Elza, (40)

Chapter 31

Arturs and Elza were told by the Immigrant Inspector that the plan had been changed. They were no longer going to the farm in Illinois. They would be placed on a train in the morning to Colden, New York. A Lutheran church would be sponsoring them. They would not be working on a farm after all. Kitija was most delighted! She hoped that Colden was a large city!

After World War Two, The United States of America admitted 205,000 refugees. Of these, 47,000 were Latvians. They were admitted into the country under the "Displaced Persons Act." This act helped those individuals who were victims of persecution by the Nazi government or who were fleeing persecution based on race, religion, or political opinions. These individuals were granted permanent residency and employment without making someone give up their job. The displaced person could bring their family with them as long as they were "good" citizens who could stay out of jail and provide financially for themselves without public assistance. The spouse and children under twenty one were eligible for permanent residency. A child who was under the age of sixteen who became an orphan because their parents went missing or died would also be cared for by the U.S.

Boarding the train this time could not have been more different from the time before. Elza felt like she might burst with happiness. The excitement, while waiting in line to board the train, could be seen in every adult's face. It could be heard in the laughs and squeals from the children holding onto their parents' hands. Elza looked at her three young girls. Their eyes glistened, heads filled with pictures of how their lives would unfold from this moment forward. It was quite a rare moment indeed. Most families do not experience one large leap into their future together. This is what it felt like as Elza stepped onto this train. Relief, joy, and anticipation overwhelmed her as she sat down. The whistle blew announcing the beginning of the rest of their lives.

This foreign land passed quickly from just beyond their windows. It was ever changing, with a backdrop of many foreign languages happily chattering throughout their train car.

When they were told they would be getting off at the next stop, Arturs quickly double checked his family's paperwork in his shirt pocket. Elza checked her pocket as well. It was still safe in her dress folds. The prayer that had been part of so many painful moments now had brought her family to freedom. Everyone descended down the stairs, with no possessions, ahead of Arturs. Elza walked up to Arturs as he stepped onto the solid ground. She wrapped her arms around his neck and gave him a kiss. "Happy Birthday Arturs!" She knew there could never be a better gift than the one he received on his forty-fifth birthday.

Arturs, Inara, Elza, and Olita, Colden, N.Y.

Chapter 32

Pastor Kleindinst and George Miller, a church member, were at the station to meet this homeless family. Elza had practiced a few sentences in English on the train. "Sank-you! Ve are so heppy you take us. Ve ken hep you so much!!" Pastor Kleindinst immediately knew they'd made the correct decision. The congregation would flood them with love and encouragement. He could hardly wait until they could meet them!

Colden was a small country town south of the city of Buffalo, New York. It was not unlike Gulbene with its rolling hills, flowers, and small town feel. Everyone knew each other and they also seemed to know about this small family's arrival. There was one church in town, the Lutheran Church, which was sponsoring them.

At first, it was a bit overwhelming for all of them, not speaking or understanding English. There were also times when the misunderstanding was met with laughter on both sides. For instance, during one early conversation, Arturs tried telling Pastor Kleindinst about the "dusty" (he meant nasty) people from the train in Germany. Pastor Kleindinst relayed the information to his wife. She promptly gathered her dusting supplies and walked over to the Nogobods family, in the small apartment behind the church where they were staying. At first Elza was upset that Arturs could have complained about the cleanliness of this beautiful apartment. How embarrassing! However, once they realized the misunderstanding, they all laughed whole-heartedly!

The church family encircled their family with love. They took up collections of food and clothing to help get the family started. Each Sunday after church they would go down to the basement to gather all the donations. Kitija and Inara especially loved this. Elza would take the clothes they received and take them apart to make new dresses from the materials. A member of the church, George Miller, very generously loaned their family his apartment. The apartment had two bedrooms and a kitchen with an electric stove! There was a bathroom with flushing toilets and sinks with running water! The best, however, was the bathtub. Here you could soak in warm water and cover yourself with the lather from the most sweet smelling bars of soap! Life in Colden was even more delightful than could ever have been imagined.

The girls began attending school and would practice their English words they were learning with their grandmother and parents. If a fly landed on the table while they ate, they would each blurt out, "Flee, free!" or "fly!" until the girls were satisfied with their answers and pronunciation. This is how they all learned the English language. Except for Arturs, who claimed to know five languages; Latvian, German, Russian, English, and Japanese! When we questioned him about Japanese, he'd say, "I knowum one word in Japanese! That countum! I tellum you!" He actually created his own language, and it was forever known as "Papa's language." If he was trying to tell you something using his broken English, and you didn't understand, he would ask, "What langmich you speakum?" He once told Inara, "I have dos problem. I not yet learn English and I forgotum Latvian!"

Elza and Kitija worked by cooking and cleaning for the Booth family. Arturs was able to find work on a nearby turkey farm. Berta had meals ready for everyone when they returned to the apartment. Life was good. Arturs continually worked to get Anna and Indulis to the U.S. About one year later, with George Miller's help, Anna and Indulis arrived! A feast of turkey, salads, and pies awaited their arrival on the kitchen table, and fresh daisies in a mason jar gave the table a fresh touch! The celebration was spent partially catching up on what they had missed during the previous year and partially answering questions about this new life in America.

Arturs Nogobods' Language
Recalled by Jesse Meyer 8/08/2015

"You make me big head!" ("You're giving me a headache!")
"I no cheese!" ("I'm not cheating at Checkers!")
"I make stake." ("I made a mistake.")
"You like kisses?" ("Would you like a Hershey's kiss?")
"You understand what I say? Won kinda langmich you speakum? Hungarian?" ("Do you understand me? What kind of language do you speak? Hungarian?")

"You looks for trouble, I findum for you boy." (If you were looking for trouble, he was ready for you.)

"Eir it's lousy boy. But sometimes eir ok" ("You're a bad boy, but sometimes you're good.")

"Kibbie ist strong man. Allie just run round and round and round. Hap hours. Make me crazy." (His commentary on taking the two dogs (Kibbie and Allie) out for a walk. Kibbie does his business immediately. Allie just sniffs around for a half hour making Arturs crazy.)

"You make me picture?" ("Are you filming me?")

"Me latta time." ("I have lots of time before I have to do that chore.")

"Me no time." ("I've run out of time and can't do that chore.")

"Nu? Sick Stomach?" ("Stomachache?")

"Won kinda man you no drink 10 o'clock beer? Garbache son-in-law" (You are a 'garbage' son-in-law for not drinking beer at 10am.)

"Zon left hand scratches, money come in. Zon right hand scratches, money go out." (Superstition; acquiring or losing money depending on which hand itches.)

"Sometime I findum money Treiman home." (Sometimes he'd find money, when helping with the wash, while visiting Kitija Treimanis' home.)

"Gred outa here!" ("Get out of here!")

"I tellam you how to pickam up rabbits na wintertime. Rabbits na wintertime ist very hungry for bitamin. Eir pickam up onion, eyes froze up...pickam up rabbits." ("I will tell you how to catch a rabbit in the wintertime. Rabbits during the

Winter are very hungry for vitamins. You put an onion on the snow. Rabbit picks up the onion, and his eyes tear up and then freeze over. Then you just pick rabbit up!")

"I tellam true store." "(I'm telling a true story.")

"Sometimes girls lil too much meat." ("That woman is too heavy for my liking.")

"Nu? Dresses up?" ("Hey, you look nice today.")

"I smart na school."("I was smart in school.")

"Alls ok? Ok, bye." (Once a day he would call and ask if everyone was ok? Satisfied, he would hang up.)

Chapter 33

In 1953, the Nogobods family was able to build a small house in Orchard Park, New York. The house was set back from the main road. It had a small cozy porch on the front of the house made from field stones. There were rows of lilac bushes as tall as trees in every color along the south side of the house. This fragrant line divided the property. On cool spring mornings, the sheer curtains covering the window in Berta's bedroom would billow to allow the fragrance of lilacs to awaken her soul.

In the backyard, Arturs and Elza planted three apple trees. They also had a bee colony from which they could always have fresh honey. There was a beautiful flower garden across the middle of the backyard with flowers in every color and size, a feast for the senses. The opening in the middle of the garden allowed one to walk past the apple trees to the very back of their property. This was where rows of vegetables and herbs grew with seemingly little effort. All parties during the summer (and there was always something to celebrate) would be held in this backyard. Everyone fought over the favorite seat under an arch of deep purple grapes, on the north side of the backyard. It was at one of these parties that Anna started to take notice of Aleks Siraks. He had lived in Gulbene and had met with the family many times in the camps as he was a friend of Arturs. He was a handsome man with a smile that accentuated his dimples. He lived initially in Connecticut, where he had found a sponsor. Later he moved about an hour away where he'd begun working in Rochester, New York. Anna noticed he had always played with Indulis and kept him giggling when he was around. This in turn made her smile. Finally smiling again felt good!

Arturs in window, Aleks Siraks on bottom left.

At one such party, Aleks asked Anna on a date. She accepted, and finally, happiness snuck its way back into her heart. Aleks was a good man. He was a hard working family man. She very much enjoyed her time with Aleks. Indulis seemed to feel the same! Six months later, on February 27, 1954, they were married. They moved their little family into the city of Buffalo where Indulis attended school.

The house in Orchard Park looked and smelled like home. It was a home without boundaries, where you could speak as you wished without penalty. You were free to become anything you dreamt of. Kitija dreamt of going to college or maybe design school. Elza, however, told her she would need to educate herself in something she could use to support herself. She decided on beauty school where she could learn, among other things, to cut and style hair. She would need to work a full-time job at the dry cleaners near Aunt Anna to pay for her night school. Since the school was in the city, she needed to stay with Anna and Aleks during the week. She only returned to Orchard Park on the weekends. While living in the city, she attended many Latvian get togethers. During one of these parties, Kitija noticed she had caught the eye of Janis Treimanis. He told her she was the most beautiful girl he'd ever seen! He announced, "Someday you will marry me!"

Arturs found a job in the city of Buffalo at a factory that manufactured boxes. Elza worked at a factory where they made wooden pallets. In the evenings she scrubbed pots and pans at the Orchard Park Country Club. She eventually worked at the Fisher-Price toy factory working on the assembly line. It was here on this assembly line that she met Anna Neidermier. They became best friends quickly. They were both interested in gardening and baking. They laughed together a lot, and this made the time working on the assembly line pass quickly.

Inara met Janet Overfield in high school. She was a very pretty blond-haired girl with blue eyes. They both had a bit of mischief in their eyes. They stayed good friends through the years. She had a brother with blue-green eyes and long eyelashes. He was handsome in his white tee shirt and jeans and very funny. He'd captured her attention! Lately, Inara noticed, even though he was older by two years, he was around more and more when she was working on homework with Janet. Janet was not willing to share her best friend, and tried her best to keep Billy out of their way.

Orchard Park, N.Y. Arturs, Inara, Berta, Elza, and Anna sitting in chair.

Orchard Park, N.Y., Berta

Orchard Park, N.Y. Inara posing on the snow bank, while Berta shovels snow.

Orchard Park, N.Y. From left: Kitija, Elza, Inara, and Olita in front.

Chapter 34

Christmas Eve of 1954 was extra special. It also seemed to set a precedent for Christmas Eves to come. Large snowflakes fell as Anna, Aleks, and Indulis arrived. It was icy on the dirt driveway and Arturs, true to his own made-up language, called out "carefula dolls!" As everyone arrived, they took heed. They completely understood what he was expressing! As they climbed the three concrete steps, a metal milk box waiting patiently to their left, they hung on to the railing for support. The wind was howling and drifts of snow began forming to the north side of the driveway.

As they entered the house, it felt as if a woolen blanket had engulfed them. There was an immediate wave of heat that touched their faces and soon it reached their hands and toes. Then came the greetings! Berta was dressed in red with a small early Christmas gift encircling her neck. Elza, in a flowered apron covered in splashes of flour, welcomed them into the warmth. Arturs, in a navy blue sports coat, took the gifts and hurriedly closed the door behind them. No one would "catchum cold" on his watch.

The girls excitedly greeted Indulis and walked into the living room to show him the Christmas tree. It stood in the corner of the small living room with several ropes keeping it perfectly in place. There was an angel on top. Elza made many hand crocheted ornaments in red, white, and blue! Stars, bells, and snowmen, complete with red hats and scarves. So many strings of colorful lights that took your eye down to many colorfully wrapped gifts. So many beautiful packages! So many ribbons floating amongst them. They seemed to begin under the tree branches and pour out of control into the living area. The small kitchen was packed with mismatched chairs gathered from all parts of the house to accommodate the family. The table was covered end to end with a feast of foods. Elza and Arturs would begin cooking and baking for this event weeks ahead of time.

There were so many aromas filling the air! The traditional Christmas Eve dinner was served in excess! Turkey, goose, ham, sauerkraut, potatoes, rasuls (a Latvian potato salad), Aukstagala (jellied pig's feet, a Latvian delicacy) and Pirags. Wine and liquor flowed easily. Eventually everyone moved into the small, cozy living room. The Christmas tree had flooded the room with its merry scent of pine. Arturs stood up ceremoniously, and led everyone in singing "Silent Night," first in English, then in Latvian. Next, the girls and Indulis sang a song of their own in front of the tree! Then and only then, each gift was passed out. When the gifts had been opened, everyone would gather again for cakes, pies, dozens of homemade Christmas cookies, coffee, and after dinner drinks! Everyone talked loudly and all at once.

Year after year Christmas Eve was always celebrated in this exact manner. It seemed to become a celebration of life, a celebration of family. Strong roots continued, and the branches of the Nogobods family tree grew longer and greener with the births of each grandchild and eventually great grandchildren! Kitija married John Treimanis and they had two sons; Edwin and Richard. Inara married William Overfield and had a daughter, Sandra (your Nonnie), and a son, Randall. Olita met Cornelius Meyer at the University of Buffalo, where they both attended classes. Cornelius spotted Olita in the library. He claims it was love at first sight! They married and had two sons, Jesse and Aaron. Indulis married Sue and had two girls, Lauren and Amy. The families continued to grow. Small fold-up tables were added to the end of the kitchen Christmas table. There also was a table set up in the bedroom. This was the "children's room!"

It was amazing to see, years later, that everyone always spent Christmas Eve engulfed in a love like no other. Maybe it was the promise Arturs had made to his papa so many years ago as they planted their tree. "The secret to its strength was in the roots and its foundation." Arturs was the one his papa had placed in charge of watering and fertilizing it. He had said, "Make me proud!" Arturs had never forgotten that day. Since the young age of thirteen, he had never fallen short on his quest.

Elza's Naturalization certificate, 4/05/1962

Arturs' Naturalization certificate, 12/07/1961

Chapter 35

Berta died in her sleep, at the age of 74. Arturs and Elza had taken care of her their entire married life. She had gone through the struggles alongside of them, and had taken an important role in their journey to safety. She had traveled far from Gulbene, and had seen countries she had only dreamt of. No doubt she slept peacefully in the end before joining the only man she had ever loved.

Anna and Aleks had saved enough money to purchase a quaint house on Lake Canisius. The lake was surrounded by houses along its banks. It was a quiet lake, where warm breezes beckoned you to take early morning rides across its shimmering silver waters. Aleks very much enjoyed fishing on his small boat and bringing home fresh fish daily. It was here on this lake where they would enjoy watching their grandchildren grow. Elza and Arturs retired and spent much of their time in Orchard Park entertaining their grandchildren. Elza would call and coax her grandchildren with promises of freshly baked jelly rolls and her "good soup!" The grandchildren nicknamed this potato soup, because in fact, it was so good and always held a surprise in it! If you were lucky enough to get a peppercorn in your soup bowl, according to Nana, you would have good luck! Anyone who has ever bitten into a peppercorn knows the awful taste on your tongue. Their Nana put the intriguing spin on it to turn it into a prize before they could turn up their noses!

Arturs met everyone who came to visit with a Hershey's chocolate kiss. He would give it to you, watch while you unwrapped it, and would take the foil and throw it out for you. This procedure never changed. It was his joy to give it to you, watch while you popped it into your mouth, and his job to throw away the wrapping. Arturs entertained the grandkids with houses he helped them make in the backyard made from boxes. He was very good at this and would even make shutters that could open and close. He had plenty of boxes he had gotten from the factory he'd worked at. The grand kids would play all afternoon in these cardboard apartment complexes, taking breaks to pick wild strawberries from the fields next to their home. They would present their strawberries to their Nana, and she would always look amazed at how many berries they had found. They would add sugar, cook them with her on her gas stove, and eat them in perfectly chipped bowls using mismatched spoons. Never has there been a sweeter treat.

Arturs always enjoyed telling the grandchildren his stories. One favorite story was that he could kill flies with an electric force in the palm of his hand! He would see a fly on the flowered plastic tablecloth that covered the kitchen table and perform for them. He would take his hand and slowly creep up on the fly, and when his palm was over the fly, he would say, "you watchum! Electric in my hand, dos fly feelum and kent move!" And in an instant he would slap his hand to the table and he always got the fly! He'd nod his head, pleased with his performance, and say "See! I tellum you! Electric!"

Chapter 36

Initially, Randy (Randall) moved to Tampa, Florida. Then in 1985, Sandra, Vincent, her husband of three years, and their 8 month old daughter, Ashlee, made the move to Jupiter, Florida. In 1986, Elza and Arturs followed Inara and Bill down to Jupiter, Florida to live out the rest of their lives in the "Sunshine State." Richard, Edwin, and eventually Kitija followed.

Elza especially enjoyed living in the warm weather and being nearer to some of her family. Olita and Cornelus raised their families in Cheshire, Connecticut, but they never missed a Christmas Eve!

On August 23, 1989, tens of thousands of demonstrators in 21 cities including New York, Seattle, London, Stockholm, Toronto, and Perth participated in "Black Ribbon Day" rallies. Two million people also joined hands in a human chain that connected the three Baltic countries; Estonia, Latvia and Lithuania. They wanted to show unity in demanding their return to independence. It covered 419.7 miles. The protesters carried radios to know exactly when to join hands. The human chain went through Vilnius to Tallinn, via Riga. They did this to draw attention to the secret Molotov Pact. This pact, with its secret protocols, had led to the U.S.S.R. occupying the three Baltic countries. This rally coincided with the 50th anniversary of Nazi Germany and the Soviet Union signing the Molotov Pact. The protests showing the dramatic human chain were broadcast all over the world. Only then would the Soviets admit there had been a secret pact. Up till then the Soviet history books reported that the three Baltic countries joined the Union voluntarily. This proved to be the first step in successfully regaining independence for all three Baltic countries. It has since become an official remembrance day in the Baltics.

Retirement in Florida was relaxing and enjoyable. Elza and Arturs could not believe how much their lives had changed over the years. Life was good! Arturs exercised every day by walking 1000 steps. He did this without fail. I once found him walking up and down the corridor in a hotel, where we were staying, counting each step! Both Elza and Arturs remained healthy and happy in their small apartment in Florida.

Arturs passed his time entertaining his great- grandchildren now. Sandra's children; Ashlee, Johnathon, and Jillian lived nearby. Randall and Kelly from Tampa would visit with three of his great-grandchildren, Mitchell, Kaelee, and Carson. Carson especially had a fondness for Nana! Edwin married a very sweet girl named Jean. Jean had always loved Nana as if she were her own grandmother. Their children, Tiffany and Alex, lived in Tampa but visited regularly. Arturs drew pictures of his house and property in Gulbene all the time and always with the bunny. Everyone was also met at the door with a chocolate kiss without fail. Arturs and Elza never traveled back to visit their homeland. Arturs told Elza they had worked so hard to get away from there and he was convinced that if they visited, they would somehow be kept there and not allowed to return. Although they would write letters to Elza's last living brother; Artvids, and the nieces, Maija, Ievina, and Ineta would come to visit them, they never saw Gulbene again. They never saw Raimonds and his family again. They often wondered where they had found sponsors. Elza always included them in her prayers. The Jaunzemis' family found sponsors in Niagara Falls, New York and the Konrads Jaunzemis' family found sponsors in Hamilton, Canada. Both were close enough to visit, and many good times were enjoyed by all throughout the years.

 They relaxed each evening in their screened-in porch. Arturs would bring coffee and place the flowered cups on the wooden table between them. Elza, always in a printed dress with a ruffled apron, would bring the napkins and coffee cake, the kind made of sugar and cinnamon, with slices of apples on top. The day was never complete without freshly baked desserts.

 They sometimes just sat next to each other enjoying the warm evening breeze. They would watch the sky turn from pinks to purples as the sun flirted with the horizon. They enjoyed each other's company without needing to have a conversation.

 Other times they would reminisce. Arturs always told Elza he knew she would marry him, right from the first time she blushed after meeting his eyes in that chorus room. Elza would give him that half smile, the kind that only showed off one dimple. All these years later, he still thought he was every school girl's dream. He still in fact made her laugh daily. They would count all their blessings over coffee and crumb cake.

In all their dreams, they could never have imagined growing old together in a quaint little seaside town called Jupiter. Each evening, as darkness marked the end of the day, they would agree. They were so fortunate in more ways than they could ever keep track of. God had truly blessed them with each other. Blessed them with family, and watched over them in order to survive the difficult times. God still blessed them now, during these peaceful evenings side by side.

Chapter 37

Arturs always said, "I live to be 101!" Elza and family joined in celebrating Arturs 90th birthday. He told everyone it was the 1,000 steps every day that got him to this special birthday. That and Elza's Pirags!

The next day, Inara took him to the family doctor. He was looking more than a bit yellow. The doctor admitted him to the hospital to conduct some testing, as he also did not like the way he looked.

The test showed a blockage, most likely a tumor. The next day he began to run a fever. The physicians tried their best, but could not find the cause of the staph infection. The fever grew higher as Arturs continued to get weaker. In 90 years he had never had the need to be hospitalized. The family was told to prepare themselves for letting Arturs go.

Kitija went with her father as they transported him to the Hospice facility where he would be more comfortable. The bright Florida sun lit up Arturs face as they wheeled him to the waiting van. Kitija kissed his cheek as she knew this would be the last time he would feel this warmth from the sun on his tired face. He blinked and smiled, squeezed her hand in reassurance. He must have known the time was nearing.

Elza and family followed them to the Hospice facility. Elza was quiet, with her shoulders back and her head held high. She would have to be strong for her family. He would expect this of her. She also knew that she would have to be the one who helped Arturs pass to the next life with her comfort.

The room was comfortable with soft yellows and blues. Elza immediately pulled the overstuffed bedside chair up to Arturs and kissed him. She held his hand and gave him a smile. This is the way she stayed, holding his hand looking into his eyes, throughout the evening and then into the night. His three daughters, grandchildren, and even Ashlee, Johnathon and Jillian, three of his great-grandchildren, came to say goodbye. Elza never took her eyes off Arturs' face. No conversation was needed between them. They knew without speaking what they each felt for the other. Well into the night Arturs' tired blue eyes closed for the last time. Elza clutched his strong, weathered hand and held it up to her heart. She knew he could hear her and she wanted him to be comforted.

> She began, «Sonaki pedejo es palieku pie Tevis
> tad jaskiras, nekas Vairs nepalids
> Ka magu pieminu Ko Varu dot no sevis
> Es savu milestibu nosutu Tev lids.»

> English translation;
> "Tonight is the last night we will spend together.
> We have no choice but to separate.

No one can help us.
As a small remembrance of me...
Take my love with you."

Elza repeated this over and over to make sure he heard these words of love until he could no longer stay.

Just before dawn Anna awoke from a dream. She saw her brother walking into the ocean. When Arturs saw her he turned around and waved...

Arturs' long journey had come to an end. He was laid to rest next to Berta, on top of a hill in Colden. He was buried with a bag of Hershey's chocolate kisses.

Elza sat alone on her screened porch. Everyone of course came to visit, but you could see she felt alone. She still sat on her lounge chair, watched the sun setting, but her smile was gone.

I asked her what I could do to help. She said "Nothing, I just don't feel comfortable enjoying my life if Papa isn't here with me." I told her, "Papa would want you to move on. He would want you to enjoy your great grandchildren!" She looked at me not convinced.

A few days later I had a dream. Nana and her great grandchildren were on top of a wagon. It was being pulled by two horses. I was in the bushes watching and they were riding right past me. Nana was laughing with the children, clearly enjoying herself. Then I noticed Papa was sitting behind them. They looked like they weren't aware of him sitting there. He was smiling at the scene he was observing. All of a sudden, he looked straight at me in the bushes and smiled as he gave me a nod!

I couldn't wait to tell Nana about my dream! When I did, she seemed to take it as a sign. A sign that she still had so much to give. A sign also that Papa would want her to go on living her life to the fullest!

Chapter 38

Nana's last living brother, Arvids, died in 1996, leaving behind his wife, Erna and all five of his children and their families. He and his family had only enjoyed freedom in his homeland for a brief time. We all saw the letter but couldn't imagine the heartache she must have felt. He had only a short time to enjoy a Free Latvia. President Clinton became the first president to visit any of the Baltic countries. When in Riga, he said "Briviba! Vabadus! Laisve!" FREEDOM!" Russia officially ended its military presence in the Baltics in August of 1998 by decommissioning the "Skrunda-1" radar station in Latvia. The last soldier left Baltic soil in October of 1999.

Finally, there would not be letters from their nieces in Latvia that were written in code. Until now knowing that the mail was being looked at, they would have to use code phrases. One such phrase would be "the flour man was late again." That would tell Elza that they didn't have a lot to eat.

In June of 2002, Elza's three daughters and four of her grandchildren visited Latvia. It was free now and travel was easy. We were met at the airport by Arturs' niece, Ineta. I kept a journal that I could write my thoughts and memories in. At the time, I never knew just how important that journal would become.

When we came back, we couldn't wait to share our experiences with Nana. She enjoyed watching our expressions as we told her what she already knew. Her homeland was beautiful, filled with her beautiful family.

Anna Siraks fell ill and went to join her big brother on July 10, 2002 just after we returned from Latvia. She and Uncle Aleks had a wonderful life together. Aleks took Anna's ashes and moved to a small town just outside of Gulbene. He lived a full year with his niece there before he also died. Anna and Aleks Siraks are both buried side by side in the Latvian countryside.

In June of 2005, I asked my daughters if they would like to join us on a second trip. Ashlee and Jillian, along with my mother and aunts took a girls trip to Latvia. Before we left, I asked "Nana, what would you like us to bring back for you?" Without hesitation she said, "Three small pebbles from my homeland."

We called Nana from her childhood home where some of Arvids family still lived. We were so excited to share our experiences with her, from her own kitchen in Gulbene! After gathering her composure, she asked, "But did you get me those three pebbles?"

When we arrived home I brought her the pebbles. She was sitting in Papa's old brown recliner, anticipating my visit. She was wearing a pale pink dress with the flowered scarf I had bought her for Christmas. Her beautiful silver hair was combed into soft waves that touched her cheeks. Her face was wrinkled, each line giving a hint of the life she had lived. I gave her a big hug and placed the cloth with her gift into her fragile hands. I watched her as she carefully unwrapped it. She rolled the three small pebbles around and around in the palm of her hand. She said nothing but looked at them as if they were precious jewels.

As I watched her do so, I began to feel I finally understood the meaning of life.

To my Nana, life wasn't about all the material things we covet so highly in our society today. Our concept of the fairy-tale family is not something that makes a person happy according to Nana. It was all about love and happiness that life affords to those who work hard and care for their loved ones.

Nana lived a long and hard life, but as hard as it was, her life was a simple one characterized by love and devotion to her entire family. She never longed for a fancy car or a big house. The most precious gift you could give her was kind words. Nana taught us how to give unconditional love by her example. That, according to Nana, was the very essence of life. We all consider ourselves incredibly fortunate to have experienced a person so genuine and wise.

Chapter 39

Nana passed away on June 9, 2006. She was buried with the three small pebbles from her homeland. Nana's life had come full circle. Her life was a wonderful journey that touched the hearts and minds of all those who knew her.

My granddaughter, Cora, looked up at me. Her brother was fast asleep. She said, "Nonnie, your Nana sure sounds special! I wish I could have met her!"

I gave her a big hug, trying to hide my tears and said, "I think you just did."

Although she is sorely missed, every time I smell fresh baked banana bread or the coffee cake with the apples on top, her memory comes flooding back to life.

I know it must have been hard to leave us, but I like to imagine Papa was up there waiting to greet her, with a foil wrapped chocolate kiss. And if I know my Papa, he asked, "What taket you so long doll?"

"To Those I Love And Those Who Love Me"

When I am gone, release me, let me go,
I have so many things to see and do,
You mustn't tie yourself to me with tears
Be thankful for our beautiful years.
I gave you my love, you can only guess
How much you gave me in happiness.
I thank you for the love you each have shown,
But now it's time I traveled alone.
So grieve a while for me, if grieve you must,
Then let your grief be comforted by trust.
It's only for a time that we must part,
So bless the memories within your heart.
I won't be far away, for life goes on,
And if you need me, call and I will come.
Though you can't see or touch me, I'll be near,
And if you listen with your heart, you'll hear.
All my love around you soft and clear,
And then, when you must come this way alone,
I'll greet you with a smile, and say "Welcome Home"
Absent from the body: present with the Lord.

by Fawn Donaldson

Sito sutat atpanal.

Elza's favorite poem. Her handwriting at the bottom asks for it to be returned to her.

Arturs and Elza's last picture together.
In loving memory of Arturs and Elza Nogobods

The Nogobods Family Tree

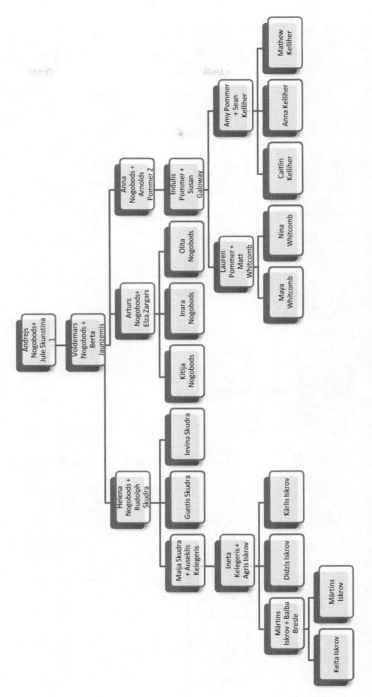

[1] Andrejs and Jule had nine children; one of who was Voldemars.
[2] Later married Aleksandis Siraks

The Zagars Family Tree

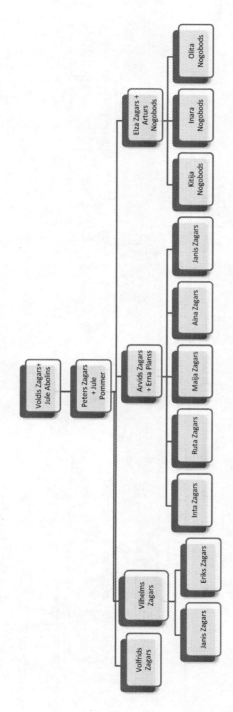

The Arturs and Elza Nogobods Family Tree

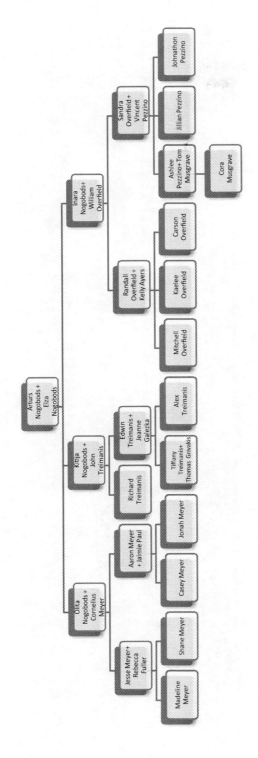

The Jaunzemis Family Tree

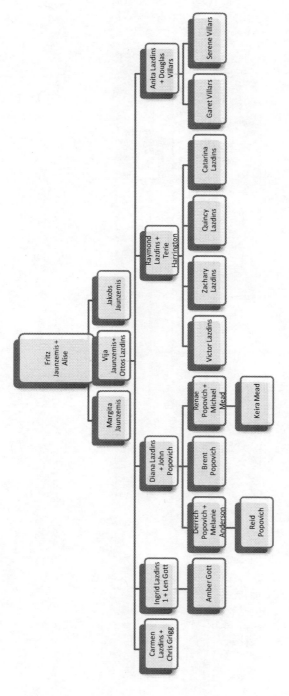

[1]Rachelle Colangelo was Ingrid's daughter from a previous marriage.

The Jaunzemis Family Tree Continued

Arturs' cousins; Milda, Fritz, Roberds, and Rita had a mother who was tragically struck by lightning in her home. Their father remarried and had another child named Konrads.

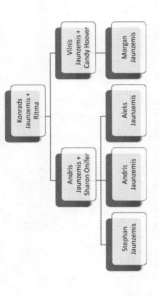

Printed in the United States
By Bookmasters